Saint Louis in the Gilded Age

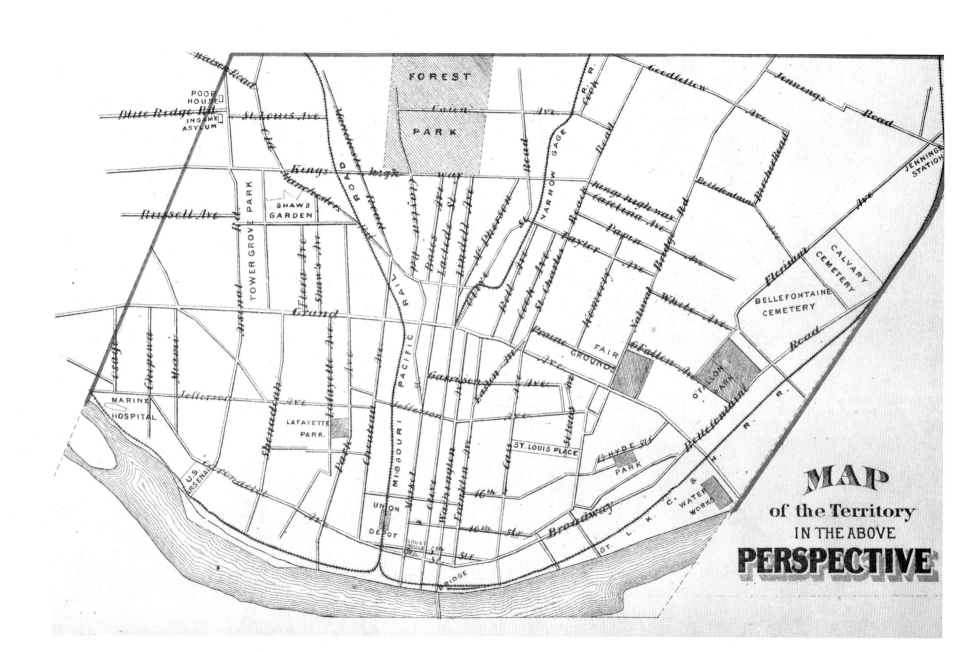

MAP
of the Territory
IN THE ABOVE
PERSPECTIVE

Saint Louis
IN THE
Gilded Age

Katharine T. Corbett
Howard S. Miller

PRESS MISSOURI HISTORICAL SOCIETY

Missouri Historical Society Press • Saint Louis

© 1993 by The Missouri Historical Society Press
All rights reserved.
The Missouri Historical Society Press
P.O. Box 11940, Saint Louis, Missouri 63112-0040

Library of Congress Catalog Card Number 93-79982

Saint Louis in the Gilded Age
ISBN 1-883982-01-4
First Edition

Printed in U.S.A. by Fiedler Printing Company,
St. Louis, Missouri
Designed by Robyn Morgan

Cover: Detail, Plate 6, *Pictorial St. Louis*, 1876. MHS-L.
Brass inkwell, c.1874. MHS-MC.
Cabinet-card photograph of an unknown St. Louisan, c.1880. MHS-PP.
Back Cover: Wine goblets, c.1870. MHS-MC.

1. **Frontispiece:** Map of the area of St. Louis depicted in *Pictorial St. Louis*, 1876.

Contents

The Missouri Historical Society's exhibition *Saint Louis in the Gilded Age* would not have been possible without the extraordinary generosity of the:

National Endowment for the Humanities, a federal agency
Metropolitan Zoological and Museum District of St. Louis

Major support was also provided by:

> Southwestern Bell Foundation
> BSI Constructors, Inc.
> Fox Family Foundation
> Mary Ranken Jordan and Ettie A. Jordan Charitable Foundation
> Laclede Gas Company
> Monsanto Fund
> Sverdrup Corporation
> Missouri Historical Society Members, Year-End Streetcar Appeal

Additional gifts have been received from:

> Miss Adelaide Cherbonnier
> Commerce Foundation
> Harry Edison Foundation
> Falcon Products, Inc.
> ITT Commercial Financial Corporation
> William T. Kemper Foundation, Commerce Bank, Trustee
> Lesley C. Knowles
> Spencer T. and Ann W. Olin Foundation
> H. Meade Summers, Jr.
> Norman J. Stupp Foundation, Commerce Bank, Trustee

Foreword

Those of us here now, on the cusp of a new century, are the legatees of St. Louis in the Gilded Age. Arbitrarily fixed as the years from 1869 to 1893, the Gilded Age was when much of the United States endured the throes of rapid urban population growth, massive industrialization, and a revolution in lifestyle. It was the period when machines, not nature, increasingly determined the pattern of life for Americans. Urban and rural dwellers alike yielded control of their livelihoods to impersonal market forces; farmers incurred debt while urban workers formed labor unions and politicians succumbed to corruption, influenced by the extreme wealth held by the few.

There were no governmental safety nets to protect citizens, and only gradually did government at any level accept responsibility for urban infrastructure and service—sewers, water, streets, bridges, and public health. By present-day standards, government was very small, with limited responsibility. This was in keeping with the American tradition of self-sufficiency, developed in tandem with a predominantly rural nation but ill-suited for burgeoning cities. New values and redefined institutions were necessary in industrial cities where populations were diverse and people depended upon each other for life's necessities yet remained strangers. American cities were sharply stratified in the Gilded Age. "Just off the boat" was a term of derision hurled at immigrants. Racial, ethnic, and religious distinctions were pervasive, and the rights of women were severely circumscribed.

St. Louis' Gilded-Age debates and decisions are now our legacy. The Eads Bridge was constructed and became St. Louis' symbol. St. Louis City and St. Louis County permanently separated, and the construction of street railways encouraged population movement to the west in an ongoing process of suburbanization. The city purchased and established Forest Park and constructed a massive system of sewers and drains which are now crumbling and must be repaired. The physical legacy of Gilded-Age St. Louis to the modern city is enormous and inescapable.

More important than our recognition of this physical legacy, however, is our discussion of the past. Through our debates, we expand our understanding of who we are, and we continue to consider the enduring issues of fairness and justice. All of this informs our decisions for our common future.

In this volume, Kathy Corbett and Dick Miller initiate that discussion about St. Louis in the Gilded Age. I know they will feel they have succeeded if their work sparks new ideas and debates. For me and for this institution, the authors have provided the basis for fresh consideration of our city, its past and its future. For this gift, I thank them.

Robert R. Archibald
President, Missouri Historical Society

Preface

In 1876 Richard Compton and Camille Dry published *Pictorial St. Louis: A Topographical Survey Drawn in Perspective A.D. 1875*, the most detailed bird's-eye view of an American city ever published. For years St. Louisans have been captivated by its stunning images of street scenes and structures, which invite comparisons between the city then and now. *Saint Louis in the Gilded Age* draws on the visual power of *Pictorial St. Louis* to evoke the past in relation to the present. This book appears in conjunction with a major exhibition on late 19th-century St. Louis history at the Missouri Historical Society.

In 1764 French fur traders established St. Louis near the mid-point of North America's greatest river system. Until the Civil War the city was the undisputed Gateway to the West, an outfitting center for regional settlers and overland travelers, and the major river port for half the continent.

During the post-Civil War years St. Louis became a major manufacturing center as well as a commercial entrepôt. Industrialism altered the size, appearance, and character of the community, and reordered the personal lives and social relations of its people. *Saint Louis in the Gilded Age* describes and strives to explain this momentous urban growth and social change by emphasizing three interrelated historical themes: the collective impact of individual choice; the importance of place; and the persistence of the past.

In his recent study of Gilded-Age Pittsburgh, Samuel P. Hays noted that urban Americans "came to want new things, to create a future different from their past, to realize new human aspirations.",In St. Louis, as in Pittsburgh, opportunities were relatively open for some residents, but for others constrained by the bounds of class, race, ethnicity, age, and gender. Whether civic leaders or ordinary citizens, St. Louisans had to select from the choices available to them; taken in aggregate, their daily private decisions had profound and lasting public consequences.

If choice directed the historical action, geography defined the historical stage. Every event happens somewhere in particular, and it is the particulars of place—the physical and cultural geography of setting and locale—that gives the past tangible context and meaning. Camille Dry's richly detailed urban views convey a spacial immediacy that heightens historical awareness.

Much of Gilded-Age St. Louis still persists: not only in material remains, but also in attitudes, values, and expectations that have carried over from those times to ours. Issues that confronted Gilded-Age St. Louisans—the meanings of progress, of fairness, of social responsibility—remain as urgent now as they were a century ago.

The first section of this book, "The Great Metropolis of the Mississippi Valley," is an overview of St. Louis in the Gilded Age that follows the main themes of the exhibition.

The second section, "Looking Backward," takes the exhibit as its point of departure, but strives to make *Pictorial St. Louis* an even more useful guide to past times by exploring its imagery of past places. Twenty-four visual case studies are grouped into five thematic sections. Each analyzes a scene from *Pictorial St. Louis* in the light of other contemporary maps and graphics. Hopefully, these complementary, comparative perspectives—images set against words, space set against time—will illustrate how much historians have to learn from geographers.

Both the exhibition and this accompanying book were collaborative efforts, and the entire staff of the Missouri Historical Society deserves credit for seeing both projects to completion. Robert Archibald, MHS president, and the Board of Trustees were supportive throughout. Special thanks go to Patricia L. Adams, interpretation coordinator, and to Carolyn Gilman, director of exhibitions and design. The interpretation is as much Pat's as it is ours; Carolyn not only made the exhibit actually happen, but also offered valuable interpretive and editorial advice. Marsha Bray, MHS vice-president, held the whole project together with grace and persistence. Suzanne Stolar, director of development, secured funding in the community.

Members of the curatorial staff, having just inventoried and moved their entire collections, still found the strength to help select, conserve, interpret, and install artifacts and images. Thanks to all, but especially Beth Rubin, Sharon Smith, Anne Woodhouse, Sharon Fivel, Martha Clevenger, Emily Miller, Duane Sneddeker, Nicola Longford, Magdalyn Sebastian, and Peter Michel. Jim Powers and the community programs staff developed engaging exhibit-related activities. Whitney Watson, exhibit designer, and Becki Huntley, Andrew Spaulding, Robert Heard, Julie Harding, Michael Miksicek, and Caitlin McQuade of the exhibit and design staff worked wonders on a tight schedule. Kirsten Hammerstrom and David Schultz helped assemble and copy hundreds of images. Interns Lawrence Low, Chris Walker, Shirley Solomon, Lamira Martin, Julia Nicholet, Lorrie Calabrese, and Allison Phillipe, and volunteer Phyllis Weidenbaum gave valuable assistance. Robyn Morgan's graphic design made the book look better than we could have hoped. Candace O'Connor, Bettye Dew, Lee Schreiner, and David Miles carefully edited both the book and the exhibit labels. Eric Sandweiss, director of the MHS research center, Karen Goering, MHS executive vice-president, and Kathy Petersen were thorough and thoughtful readers. Andrew Hurley and Gerda Ray, MHS exchange scholars from the University of Missouri-St. Louis, shared their scholarship.

The Missouri Historical Society is grateful to the National Endowment for the Humanities for their support and for making it possible for us to draw on the knowledge and insights of several distinguished consultants. Professors David Roediger, Susan Strasser, George Lipsitz, and James Lemon were both critical and supportive.

During the twenty-some years we have researched and taught the history of St. Louis, we have often bemoaned the fact that the city has benefited from less historical scholarship than other cities of comparable age, size, and significance. St. Louis is a place we are just beginning to understand. *Saint Louis in the Gilded Age* will be successful if it encourages others to join in the collective and urgent effort to study and debate where this community came from, and where it might be going.

Katharine T. Corbett, director of interpretation
   Missouri Historical Society

Howard S. Miller, professor of history emeritus
   University of Missouri-St. Louis

July, 1993

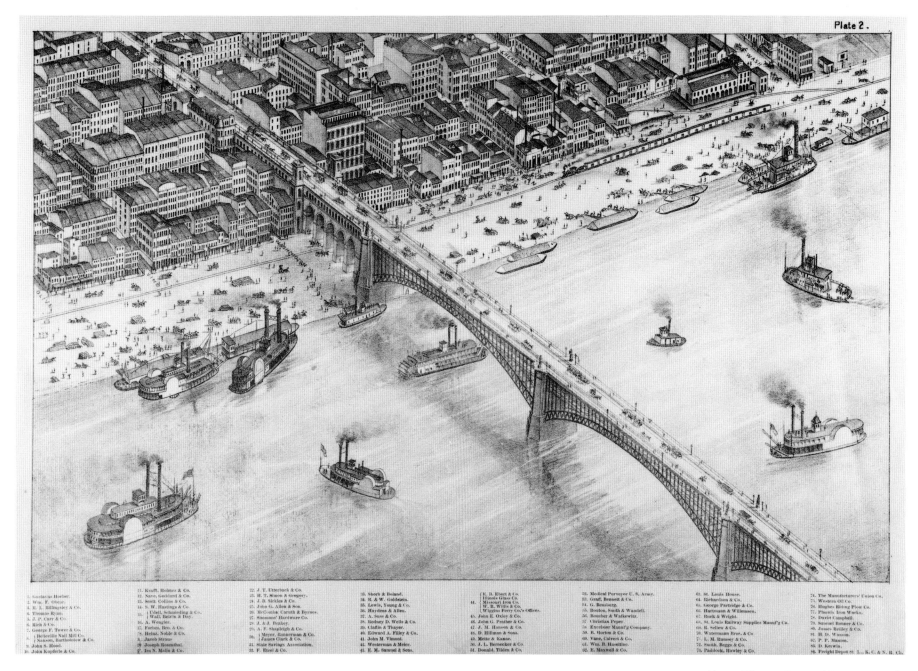

Plate 2.

1. Gustavus Hoeber.	11. Krafft, Holmes & Co.	22. J. T. Utterback & Co.	33. Shorb & Boland.	E. B. Ebert & Co.	52. Medical Purveyor U. S. Army.	63. St. Louis House.	74. The Manufacturers' Union Co.

Above: Plate 2, *Pictorial St. Louis*, 1876

SAINT LOUIS IN THE GILDED AGE

THE GREAT
METROPOLIS
OF THE
MISSISSIPPI
VALLEY

3. Right: James B. Eads (1820-1887), a self-taught engineer and entrepreneur, salvaged wrecks from the bottom of the Mississippi River and built Civil War ironclad gunboats before constructing the Eads Bridge. A St. Louis booster, he adopted "Drive on" as his personal motto.

The Future Great City of the World

*St. Louis! St. Louis! we echo
    the name,
Repeated by them as the city
    of fame,
On the banks of that river
    whose waters embrace
The largest facilities known to
    the race;
The central point in its
    beautiful vale,
To which, up its waters, large
    traffic must sail.*

—Rebecca Morrow Reavis,
"The Future Great City of the World: St. Louis," 1883

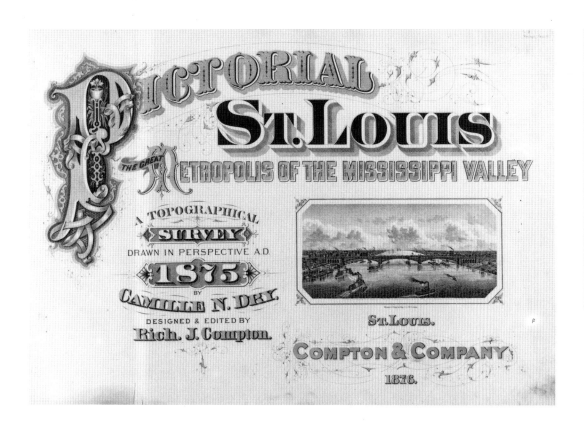

4. Above: Richard Compton bound Camille Dry's 110 drawings of St. Louis as a handsome volume, accompanied by text promoting the city and its future promise.

5. Above Right: Eads' novel bridge design required masonry piers sunk deep to bedrock. During construction, cables and scaffolding suspended the alloy steel arch tubes so that boats could pass underneath. The tubes joined to form the arches supporting the road and train decks.

The post-Civil War decades were times of unprecedented economic growth, industrial expansion, and urban development. Glittering wealth and prosperity, however, often masked the harsh underlying realities of poverty, cynicism, and despair. Mark Twain and Charles Dudley Warner named the era in 1873 when they published their satirical novel, *The Gilded Age: A Tale of Today*, which mocked material success by exposing its core of greed and corruption. In fact, the period between 1865 and the early 1890s was probably no more corrupt or hypocritical than other times, but the name "Gilded Age" stuck to this era alone, highlighting the contrasts between truth and illusion, wealth and want, that accompanied urban growth in the industrial age.

Like other Gilded-Age American cities, St. Louis was a place of contrasts and extremes that set progress against poverty, confidence against doubt, and celebration against disappointment. Social change created opportunities for some people as it dashed hopes for others. While possibilities were relatively open for the favored few, other St. Louisans had to seize opportunities within the bounds of class, race, ethnicity, age, and gender. In society, as in Darwinian Nature, there were more losers than winners.

The defining relics of Gilded-Age St. Louis are a book and a bridge. In 1875 Richard Compton, a local publisher, joined with Camille Dry, an itinerant artist, to produce *Pictorial St. Louis*, an astounding bird's-eye view that displayed the vital interplay between space, place, and people in an emergent industrial metropolis.

6. Left: Boosters and journalists encouraged St. Louisans to call the city "The Future Great." The slogan appeared with an image of the Eads Bridge on this decorative souvenir flask produced by the Anna Pottery, Anna, Illinois.

7. Below Left: Using an image of the Eads Bridge in advertisements for St. Louis products served two functions: It associated the supplier with modern marketing and rail distribution, and it promoted the bridge as a symbol of the city.

8. Far Left: Eads Bridge workmen presented this brass inkwell, adorned with engineering symbols, to James B. Eads. Pressing a lever engaged a set of gears and opened the inkwell's lid.

The previous year James B. Eads, a local entrepreneur, had forever changed the city's spatial dynamics by completing its first bridge across the Mississippi River. Compton dedicated *Pictorial St. Louis* to James Eads and used the image of the bridge as the book's frontispiece and title-page illustration.

The close timing of the two projects and their overlapping themes were more than coincidental. Both were aspects of a broader effort to make civic dreams come true. During the post-Civil War decade, local businessmen and publicists conjured up a grand vision of St. Louis as "The Future Great City of the World." The bridge was to be its economic lifeline and civic icon, the book its portrait album and showy ad.

Both artifacts embodied all the business optimism and civic glitter Gilded-Age St. Louis had to show, but neither could usher in an urban golden age—or even recover the mercantile glories St. Louis had previously known. Before the Civil War, St. Louis had prospered as the region's principal river port. By the 1850s the city was already losing much of its former geographical advantage to the railroads, which were then criss-crossing the eastern prairies and beginning to bridge the Mississippi and compete for western trade. Meanwhile, the nation's main axis of economic and political power had shifted decisively northward from the old Philadelphia-St. Louis corridor to a new New York-Chicago axis. New York had already replaced Philadelphia as the nation's largest city and major port; Wall Street had replaced Chestnut Street as the principal money market; and the rural cotton South had lost political power to the urban industrial north. On the eve of the Civil War, St. Louisans lacked the civic will—and ultimately the power—to reverse such broad shifts in national life. While upstart Chicago seized regional

initiative as a railroad center, St. Louisans merely talked about building a Mississippi River bridge. Then four years of Civil War distracted local initiative and closed southern markets. St. Louis trade collapsed. Eastern capital flowed north. Chicago surged ahead.

The Future Great City booster bombast of the early Gilded Age hardly masked the mood of civic jealousy and mounting desperation. The forces of faith and fear soon combined, however, to spark a broad-based urban renaissance. In 1874 the whole community turned out to celebrate the dedication of the Eads Bridge. Civic progress stalled during the hard times of the mid-1870s, then took off again in the '80s. By then St. Louis ranked as the fifth-largest city in the nation, with a population of 350,000, an expanding urban infrastructure, and the amenities of a modern industrial metropolis.

Gilded-Age St. Louisans in every walk of life were justifiably proud of their achievements, especially their elegant Mississippi bridge and *Pictorial St. Louis*, the nation's most stunning urban portrait. A century and a quarter later, these paired artifacts of space and place still evoke their times and invite important questions about the continuing influence of the past on the present. Gilded-Age St. Louisans lived through confusing times of material progress, grinding poverty, and social disarray. Their urge to gild and embellish and dream the impossible was a reflection of their optimism and sense of accomplishment, but also a tacit acknowledgment that surface luster could make grim realities more attractive and easier to bear.

9. Left: Mass-produced, ornate gas lamps with classical figures, such as this one from the St. Louis Merchants' Exchange Trading Room, added to the grandeur of Gilded-Age centers of capitalist power.

10. Above: Steam powered Gilded-Age industry. In 1866 Anheuser-Busch Brewery began using this 25-horse-power steam engine to run an agitator in the mash cooker of the brewery.

Engines of Growth and Change

But now the giant
Steam is king
And proves a
cruel master;
The mighty engines,
whirring, sing:
"My friend, you
must work faster."

—Program of the Milling and Flour Merchants' Annual
Excursion, St. Louis, 1888

Industrial St. Louis rose on historic mercantile foundations. New manufacturing ventures augmented—but did not replace—older commercial enterprises; railroads reinforced the ongoing river trade. These evolutionary changes produced a remarkably diversified, geographically complex urban economy. The engines of growth and change were entrepreneurial ambition, technological innovation, and the collective efforts of ordinary people.

No single industry dominated the cityscape. St. Louis was a city of a few large factories but many small shops. Some were old establishments changing with the times; others were new ventures capitalizing on technological advances, new ways of organizing and conducting business, and new methods of marketing. Even the most innovative enterprises almost always drew heavily on local resources and past experience.

11. Below: Bryan, Brown and Company manufactured shoes in St. Louis and shipped them by rail throughout the southwest trade territory. The firm had annual sales of over two million dollars in the mid-1890s when it became the Brown Shoe Co.

The key to economic progress, as James Eads often reminded the members of the Merchants' Exchange, was cheap transportation. Eads was a local hero who had devoted his whole career—first as a riverman, then as a railroad entrepreneur—to promoting more trade at lower cost. He personified the city's newly integrated river-rail transportation strategy.

The relative economics of river and rail transport depended in part on topography. Navigable rivers were few and far between, their courses meandering with the lay of the land. Railroads, however, could operate almost anywhere. On the eve of the Civil War, aggressive Chicago railroad developers had cost St. Louis its historic upper-midwest trade by serving prairie farms and country towns located far from major streams. On the eve of the Gilded Age, St. Louis railroad developers and local merchants hungry for bigger markets set out in similar fashion to capture the trade of the river-poor, but resource-rich, American Southwest.

Encouraged by the Merchants' Exchange, St. Louis firms invaded the trade territory from Arkansas to Utah and New Mexico with compelling sales catalogues, trade journals, newspaper promotions, and legions of traveling salesmen. The huge and richly illustrated Shapleigh and Simmons hardware catalogues, like Chicago's Montgomery Ward and Sears Roebuck wish-books, brought the widening world of consumer goods to every town with a depot. St. Louis wholesale grocers stocked the shelves of country stores throughout the Southwest. The Meyer Drug Company grew into the nation's largest drug firm by supplying regional pharmacists and encouraging their professional development.

The rapid increase and shifting focus of regional trade changed the internal geography of St. Louis. Downtown expanded westward. Long-established jobbers, wholesalers, and other bulk suppliers formerly housed on the levee began moving into larger and more efficient quarters served directly by rail. By the mid-1890s, the city's economic and symbolic axis had pivoted ninety degrees, creating two business districts: the older river-linked downtown paralleling the levee as far west as 7th Street; and a newer, rail-linked commercial strip running westward along Market Street from Cupples Station to Union Station, paralleling the Mill Creek Valley railyards.

New trade patterns changed old trade practices—and even the architecture of business enterprise. Inspired by railway models of efficiency, Famous Dry Goods and a number of other old, established firms remodeled their buildings to speed the internal flow of goods and information. William Barr's department store, the oldest and largest in the city, moved to the then far-western location of 6th and Olive in 1880. Like other new-style department stores, Barr's was a model of business efficiency and fashionable elegance, a retail consumption palace for women where shopping was an adventure rather than a chore.

Gilded-Age St. Louis excelled as a processing center for regional products. Northern and southern forests supplied raw material for lumber mills, furniture, and woodenware factories. Western grain passed through local elevators, western cattle through local stockyards. In the 1880s, a number of established St. Louis shoe jobbers became shoe manufacturers, exploiting ready access to leather and close proximity to expanding western markets. New plants equipped with up-to-date machinery allowed local shoe companies such as Bryan and Brown to undersell eastern manufacturers in the lucrative work-shoe market. St. Louisans also led the nation in the manufacture of such diverse products as lead paint pigments and chewing tobacco.

12. Left: Mary Deneny, a St. Louis milliner more than forty years, made this silk moiré wedding bonnet in the early 1880s in her shop at 308 N. 5th Street.

The most dramatic new processing venture was cotton compressing. St. Louis railroads commanded the trade of the cotton-growing Southwest, but conventionally baled cotton was too bulky for profitable long-distance rail transport. In the early 1870s, James Paramore established the first of several St. Louis cotton compressing plants, where powerful machinery squeezed standard soft bales

13. Above: This banner, commemorating the 50th anniversary of the St. Louis Butchers' *Verein*, is embroidered in polychrome silk. The slogan *"Einigkeit Macht Stark* [Strength through Unity] 1906"* is embroidered on the reverse side.

into dense blocks only inches high, thus dramatically increasing transportation efficiency. Cotton compressing multiplied local rail receipts and at the same time provided local jobs and generated profits. By 1880 St. Louis ranked as the third-largest cotton market in the nation and the largest inland cotton market in the world.

The success of porcelain-glazed cookware and lager beer pointed to the growth potential in new technologies and fresh marketing techniques. During the Gilded Age the Neidringhaus brothers perfected new methods for coating cooking pots and pans with a rust-proof, easy-to-clean ceramic glaze. Graniteware was the first real advance in kitchen technology since the invention of the stove. Swamped by orders, the Neidringhaus' St. Louis Stamping Company soon outgrew its North St. Louis site and moved across the Mississippi to a new company town, named Granite City in honor of its principal product.

St. Louisans had been brewing beer for local consumption since the 1820s. In the Gilded Age nearly thirty breweries exploited the city's artesian springs, cooling caves—and thirsty drinkers. The only way to boost beer sales significantly was to tap a larger number of beer drinkers; however, traditionally brewed beer spoiled quickly and did not travel well.

The beer-marketing genius of the Gilded Age was Adolphus Busch, who in 1876 introduced a new, pilsner-style lager called Budweiser. Busch envisioned a national beer market and pioneered the necessary brewing and shipping innovations to insure consistent quality and long shelf-life. With rationalized management, invasive national marketing, and saturation advertising, he transformed a local beverage of limited sales potential into "The King of Bottled Beers."

The success of Budweiser was a local example of several broad trends in national business enterprise.

Companies everywhere were consolidating, becoming larger and more efficiently managed, in an urgent effort to control costs and reduce risks. In an expansive, highly competitive free-market economy, even a marginal advantage could mean the difference between profit and loss. System and control became crucial. The cash register was invented in the 1870s; accountancy began to replace simple bookkeeping in the 1880s, and forward-looking firms installed newly perfected desk calculators and experimented with primitive data-processing.

Cycles of boom and bust were inherent features of emerging industrial capitalism, but recurrent hard times were particularly acute during the Gilded Age, a period of general deflation in which income levels dropped faster than the cost of living. Successive depressions rocked the national economy in 1873, 1881, and 1893, leading to business retrenchment, mass layoffs, and worker distress. Urban life and industrial discipline were new to many workers fresh off the farm or the immigrant boats. Living in depressed times and dependent on cash income for food and lodging, St. Louis workers struggled just to get by.

In an effort to control the unpredictable forces of industrial capitalism, Gilded-Age labor began to organize, primarily around the chronic issues of working conditions, wages, and hours. In St. Louis, where most people still worked in small shops with five or fewer employees, skilled craft unions attracted more members than the Knights of Labor, which welcomed all workers. Local workers struck often during the Gilded Age: on the average, nearly a hundred strikers were off the job every working day between 1881 and 1894. While strikers usually enjoyed popular support, they faced open hostility and occasional violence from business leaders and the rising managerial middle class.

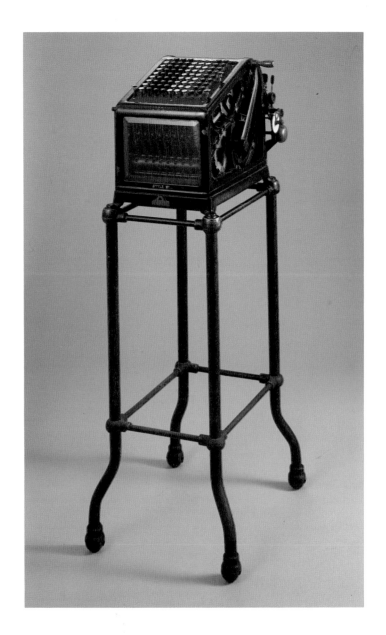

14. Left: William S. Burroughs developed his first adding machine in St. Louis in 1885. Early models, plagued with mechanical problems, have not survived. The machine shown here, made in 1903, is a model developed in 1889. Burroughs moved his American Arithmometer Company to Detroit in 1904.

15. Right: This wooden Indian stood in front of Henry Engeling's cigar store at 2037 Gravois. Stereotyped statues of American Indians identified neighborhood cigar and tobacco stores in the same way that striped poles identified barber shops.

Popular resentment boiled over in 1877, when a national railroad strike triggered a paralyzing general strike in St. Louis. For a week in late July, thousands of workers massed in the streets, shut down local businesses, and battled the authorities. Panicky officials feared a communist revolution—especially when a small but noisy local branch of the Marxist Workingmen's Party gained momentary notoriety as the loudest voice of discontent. The strike quickly collapsed, however; neither capital nor labor was ready for all-out class war. Both sides settled for an uneasy, ongoing cold war, punctuated by recurring strikes and street violence.

Women workers were doubly burdened by hard times and gender bias. Many local married women did paid work at home, typically laundry, ironing, sewing, and child care. Single women and girls more often held outside jobs, usually low-paying domestic and industrial work. The largest number of St. Louis women worked in the clothing and tobacco industries, holding down fully 15 percent of the city's total manufacturing jobs. Though they had little success, reformers worked hard to win higher pay and wider employment opportunities for women.

Capitalizing on new technologies and expanding markets, entrepreneurs and ordinary working people transformed St. Louis in the Gilded Age, spurring urban expansion and quickening the pace of social change. These engines of enterprise pushed the city beyond its limits, however, as public needs multiplied faster than public services, and mounting problems of municipal governance strained the capacity of a political system left over from an earlier age.

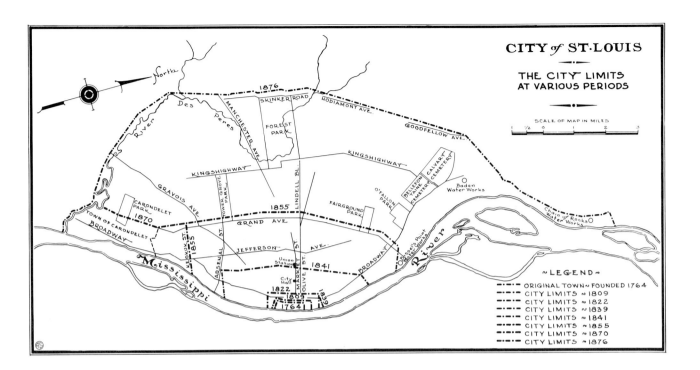

16. Above: St. Louis gradually expanded its municipal boundaries until 1876 when voters chose to triple the area of the city and separate from St. Louis County. The separation agreement for the "Great Divorce" transferred all parks within the new limits to the city.

Building the Future Great City

I think the people might as well know the limited means we have at our disposal, and then they can't expect so much to be accomplished. We have got to trim expenses to meet the revenue.

—Mayor William L. Ewing, 1882

It was easier to imagine a glittering Future Great City of the World than it was to make gritty St. Louis, Missouri, actually work. While *Pictorial St. Louis* pictured orderly urban progress, street-level reality bordered on urban chaos: growth without plan, movement without direction, parts without a whole. The problem was that a city ultimately worked together or not at all. Civic success required some degree of spatial coherence and social cohesion, even in an age that celebrated self-made individualism, free-market capitalism, and governmental laissez-faire. The essential unifying elements in expansive Gilded-Age St. Louis were municipal governance and physical infrastructure.

17. Right: The McLean Building, constructed in 1875 on the corner of 4th and Market streets, overshadowed the Old Courthouse. This ornate Second Empire office building, financed by patent-medicine manufacturer James McLean, reflected the flamboyant individualism and garish display associated with the Gilded Age.

St. Louis was a forward-looking city in a backward state, a growing metropolis within a county still largely rural. In 1870 St. Louis City was still part of St. Louis County. Although nine out of ten residents lived inside the city limits, county officials still controlled the purse strings and showed little inclination to spend county money on city needs. St. Louisans concluded that only home rule would give them command of their own destiny—political self-determination, room for expansion, an independent revenue base, more and better services at lower cost. In 1876, voters extended the city limits far (so they thought) into the country, separated irrevocably from St. Louis County, and adopted a home-rule charter. The 1877 charter authorized a Board of Public Improvements, charged with providing public infrastructure, utilities, and services within these new city boundaries.

Money, power, and legal constraints shaped the emerging pattern of city services. Creating adequate infrastructure required enormous capital investment, but the city approached its debt limit in the early 1870s. State law and city charter provisions made it practically impossible either to raise the legal debt limit or to pay it down by raising taxes.

The debt burden had important policy consequences. In the early 1870s and again in the 1890s, St. Louis spent most of its available resources on essential water and sewer services; other utilities came along slowly on a pay-as-you-go basis, or were funded privately, or had to wait. There was no simple formula for dividing infrastructure responsibilities and benefits; St. Louisans drew upon both the public and private sectors, often hopelessly mingling the two as they tied the spreading city together with networks of roads, rails, pipes, and wires. Wealthy, influential residents often took first and best advantage of new public services, or by-passed them entirely in favor of private infrastructure. Free-enterprising infrastructure development produced a multitude of private residential streets, usually with their own private sewers.

The Gilded-Age sewer system was a tangled network of public and private enterprise, an extension of a pre-Civil War system originally designed to drain polluted sinkholes and carry off storm water. With improvements, the system eventually handled both storm and waste water, but all St. Louis sewage continued to flush, untreated, into the Mississippi River. Domestic sewer service remained optional, more dependent on residents' wealth and sensibility than on their location. Although sewer lines ran through many city neighborhoods in 1880, fewer than one fifth of all homes had flush toilets. A decade later, private sewer lines from several exclusive private places in the West End discharged raw waste into the River Des Peres, converting a rustic stream into a public nuisance and fouling the air in Forest Park.

Since the 1840s, the city had assumed responsibility for water service. Most domestic users paid fixed tap and license fees for unlimited water use; heavy consumers had their water metered after 1878. St. Louis water was legendary for its muddy appearance, and it remained as turbid as ever until the turn of the century. Local defenders claimed it had more substance and character than the limpid waters of effete eastern cities; Mark Twain insisted that every tumbler held an acre of land in solution.

Cash-strapped St. Louis was never in a financial position to supply municipally owned gas, electricity, public transit, or telegraph and telephone services. Instead, the city turned these vital "public" utilities over

to private developers, luring them with long-term exclusive franchises. Utility franchises were the most valuable assets the city had to sell. The opportunities for public graft and private profit were irresistible, and franchise boodle quickly became the main currency of public corruption, compromising civic leaders, businessmen, and ward heelers alike.

Since franchise-trading and payoffs were more lucrative than actually delivering services, privately held public utility companies frequently found it profitable to overbuild in some areas and underbuild in others.

18. Above: This 1891 view from 6th Street looking west along Washington shows the expansion of the downtown business district. Electric trolleys and hanging street lights were replacing mule-drawn streetcars and gaslights. The street decorations in place for the Veiled Prophet Parade were probably illuminated by gas.

19. Above: Most streets in St. Louis were paved with gravel (macadamized) and looked like Singleton Street, located just north of Chouteau Avenue at 15th Street. Macadamized streets were usually guttered with limestone blocks before workers rolled gravel of graduated sizes onto the graded surface.

The timing, placement, and ownership of profit-driven public utilities explained much about the evolving physical shape and appearance of the city.

Streets, roads, and trolley lines were products of urban growth, but they also helped to promote it. As a spur to growth or as an expression of Gilded-Age booster optimism, the city laid out miles of streets—paved with the cheapest materials—in advance of development. Many of these half-phantom thoroughfares appeared as real streets in *Pictorial St. Louis*, making the city look even more developed than it was and thus encouraging still more investment in civic progress.

The Board of Public Improvements had formal responsibility for all public roads, but money was always scarce and funding policy favored the wealthy. Street levies were based on the assessed valuation of adjacent properties. The higher the private assessment the lower the public cost; it was relatively cheaper for the city to pave the streets of the rich than the streets of the poor. Moreover, affluent and impatient developers like those in the West End had the option of going ahead on their own, paying outright for public streets or creating whole neighborhoods of private streets maintained by adjacent property owners.

Competing private utility companies developed local public transit. Within the city, transit evolved from horse-drawn omnibuses to horse-drawn streetcars running on rails, then in the 1880s to cable and electric trolleys powered from a central station. In each case, the city's low population density focused franchise competition on the high-volume downtown routes. Since the system was driven by short-term private profit rather than long-term social planning, crowded districts soon had too much service, while remote neighborhoods had too little.

The public depended on the transit utilities, but hated their poor service, monopolistic privilege, and corrupting political influence. The most frequent and bitter strikes in Gilded-Age St. Louis were transit strikes, which grew more violent over time as companies consolidated their power and public resentment increased. Riders usually sympathized with the workers, but the owners always won.

However skewed its routings or pernicious its politics, the expanding streetcar system had profound and paradoxical effects on community social life and the shape of the city. Public transit was democratic in its tendencies: anyone could ride who had the fare, and everyone who rode shared a common urban experience and a rough social equality—even African Americans, who in 1867 successfully challenged segregated seating. Streetcars also brought to middle- and working-class St. Louisans some of the residential mobility formerly reserved for those who owned private carriages or could afford to ride suburban commuter trains.

In a densely populated city, public transit tended to draw residents together. As routes radiated outward into more sparsely settled suburbs, transit began to have the opposite effect, promoting separation and isolation. St. Louisans of every kind dispersed to take advantage of the growing array of public services and civic amenities. Areas of the city became increasingly specialized, more functionally distinct, and more differentiated by class and race.

20. Left: Transit workers drove streetcars like this small, mule-drawn "bobtail" for twelve to eighteen hours a day. In 1880 the 2,280 horses and mules that pulled St. Louis' 496 streetcars deposited twenty-three tons of manure on city streets every day.

21. Below Left: In the 1890s more businesses than homes had electrical service. The Emerson Electric Company offered blade guards as an option on fans like this one produced in 1895.

22. Above: In the 1880s a silk crazy quilt was the sign of a fashionable homemaker with the leisure to create purely decorative items. Based on a practical design that used cloth scraps to make bedcovers, these new quilts were frequently made from pre-packaged silk blocks and draped over parlor furniture.

23. Above: Furniture designs of English reformer George Eastlake became popular in the Gilded Age, offering an alternative to elaborately carved and curved Victorian pieces. Fashion-conscious consumers of moderate means could purchase new machine-made "art furniture" like this Eastlake-style chair.

24. Left: Gilded-Age home furnishings could be at once decorative, functional, and symbolic. This hand-carved plant stand expressed its owners' appreciation of Nature, as well as their wealth and taste.

25. Right: Wreaths made of human hair decorated the homes of middle-class St. Louisans and expressed family-focused sentimentality. Relatives in Austria sent hair for this wreath, created to commemorate a 25th wedding anniversary.

Private Life

Our actual enjoyments are so few and transient, that were we not blessed with homes our lot would be miserable. Every father and mother should do their utmost to make their surroundings the most inviting, the scene of neatness, arrangement and taste.

—Straus-Emerich Outfitting Co.,
Handbook and Manual, 1894

26. Above: Louisa Hackman made this artistic assemblage of wool flowers for her home. Displayed under glass, it became a family heirloom.

In the mid-1880s William Tecumseh Sherman, the Civil War general and local real estate speculator, spent at least 15,000 dollars a year maintaining his Garrison Avenue household. During those same years Andrew Fruth, a partner in a tombstone company, budgeted twelve hundred dollars annually for his middle-class home on Sidney Street. Louis Wehle, an often-unemployed laborer who probably made less than three hundred fifty dollars a year, kept up his DeKalb Street flat with the help of his wife, Clara, who took in boarders. Bridget McHale, a widow with three children who lived on North 8th Street, stayed out of the poorhouse only because the city granted her five dollars a month temporary relief.

Although Sherman was far from the richest person in St. Louis and Wehle was by no means the poorest, these two men lived in profoundly different worlds, separated not only by income but also by social class. Because class depended both upon culture and economics, class distinctions were often ambiguous. Nevertheless, Gilded-Age St. Louisans generally conceived of their society as a four-tiered hierarchy of the wealthy, the middle class, the working class, and the destitute. They accepted class divisions as facts of life, reflected in personal values, everyday behavior, and material possessions.

The home was the material possession that counted the most and best expressed class identity. Gilded-Age homes differed markedly depending upon their occupants' ethnicity, race, class, and current circumstances, but in most cases women made the decisions concerning their management and decoration.

The ideal of Gilded-Age domesticity, at least for the wealthy and the aspiring middle class, defined woman's proper place as the private world of home, man's as the public world of business and government. A spacious and well-furnished home testified to his success, a tasteful home to her refinement and determination. She saw to efficient domestic management and morally edifying embellishment; he paid the bills. Domestic servants did most of the actual work.

If they had sufficiently wealthy and generous fathers or husbands, St. Louis women could outfit their homes with all the ornate furnishings commonly associated with the Victorian era. Fashionable furniture, textiles, and endless varieties of bric-a-brac filled the parlors of the well-to-do. Buying trips to East Coast cities and European Grand Tours expanded opportunities for conspicuous consumption.

Wealth bought space and privacy in an increasingly crowded world. Family life centered in the home, but even within this haven, men and women, adults and children retreated into their separate spheres. Entry halls were ambiguous spaces—inside the structure but not quite inside the household—where family members could welcome friends, screen out strangers, and accept cards from formal callers. Parlors, dining rooms, and great halls were public rooms designed for entertaining. Living rooms were private, potentially shared family spaces, but men often retired to their libraries and billiard rooms and women to their sewing rooms, where they stitched fancy needlework and made elaborate decorative assemblages of feathers, wax, and shells. Children were supposed to be little seen and rarely heard except by the servants, who worked in plain kitchens and trod narrow back stairs to small living quarters, usually in the attic, the basement, or over the carriage house in the back yard.

Middle-class St. Louis shared many of the values of the well-to-do, but lacked the money to live in high Victorian style. Although the urban middle class expanded significantly during the Gilded Age, only about one in

ten St. Louis families had sufficient wealth to afford what later generations would regard as a middle-class home. Middle-class status was also complicated by race and ethnicity. White professionals often looked down upon their African-American counterparts, who usually earned far less but shared the same devotion to education, domesticity, and propriety. Recently arrived middle-class immigrants faced difficulties fitting in, particularly as fear of foreigners increased during the 1880s.

Home ownership was the focus of middle-class aspiration. Andrew and Caroline Fruth bought their six-room, two-story row house on the near South Side in 1876. Andrew prospered selling tombstones and was generous with Caroline's household allowance. She represented the new female shopper, the intended target

27, 28. Above: Caroline Brandenburger Fruth (1853-1958) and her husband Andrew Fruth (1849-1931) were middle-class St. Louisans who lived with their three children on Sidney Street during the Gilded Age.

29. Above: Mass production enabled some working-class families to purchase upholstered furniture like this lounge. For the equivalent of about three days of a man's pay, a homemaker could own a stylish piece to serve as both couch and bed.

30. Right: Popular, rustproof, St. Louis-made graniteware, replicated in this doll set, made housework easier but cost about three times as much as the more common tin cookware.

of consumer advertising, home-furnishing magazines, and downtown department-store promotions. Decorating and redecorating the home became almost a moral obligation, an act of family devotion and social display. Families like the German-American Fruths, proud of their ethnic heritage, might choose to surround themselves with artifacts from the old country. As ethnic St. Louisans moved up the economic ladder, however, they tended to sever their roots and assimilate the material goods and ideas of mainstream American culture.

Middle-class women were responsible for housework—shopping, cooking, cleaning, and child care—usually with the help of one female, live-in servant. Housewares advertisers cultivated both mistress and maid, publishing trade cards and other ads showing Irish and African-American servants happily cooking on new stoves or middle-class mothers teaching their daughters to sew on new machines. Improved household appliances, such as carpet sweepers and washing machines, and labor-saving gadgets, such as mechanical egg-beaters, made old chores less tedious and freed up time for still more women's work.

The high visibility of Gilded-Age wealth often obscured the fact that the vast majority of St. Louis women lacked the means to maintain a well-appointed home. The average annual manufacturing wage was just over five hundred dollars—less than a minimum-wage income in today's money. But the boundaries of working-class income and culture were imprecise; some skilled craftsmen earned more than small businessmen and office workers, and lived in homes with all the trappings of middle-class respectability. Whether they identified with—or were accepted by—their middle-class neighbors was another question.

St. Louis working-class dwellings were typically four-family flats, usually rented but sometimes owned by a resident family that let out the other apartments. Crowded with family and with boarders as well, the small rooms had scant furnishings, all functional, most second-hand. Skilled residents might build their own furniture; women did their best with little means to make their homes attractive. Thanks to Gilded-Age mass production, stylish upholstered furniture—at least one piece—was marginally affordable. For most working-class women, home was also a workplace. In addition to doing their own housework, they frequently took in laundry or lodged and fed boarders

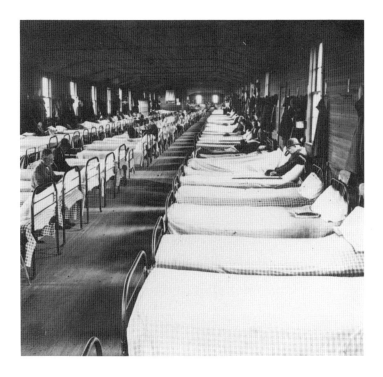

in an ongoing struggle to keep the family above the contemporary equivalent of the poverty line. Cramped quarters served double or even triple duty as living rooms, bedrooms, and kitchens. Under such conditions, space and privacy were luxuries beyond reach, cleanliness all but impossible. Members of working-class households, including children, came and went at odd hours, depending on shift schedules at work; social life went on round the clock, spilling out into the communal space of porches, sidewalks, yards, streets, and alleys.

These public spaces were also the homes of the homeless. It was easy to become a homeless person in Gilded-Age St. Louis because unskilled work was irregular and poorly paid, and employers routinely discriminated on the basis of race, age, and gender. There was no welfare system. Few people were entitled to industrial or government pensions. The needy petitioned private charities and local government for aid with no guarantee they would be found worthy of assistance.

Destitute families squeezed into rented slum housing, often alley shacks thrown up in the back yards of four-family flats, or lived day to day on the streets. A woman without a man to provide for her children could petition the city for as much as five dollars a month in public assistance, leave her children for a time in a church-supported orphanage, or ask that they be admitted to the House of Refuge, a city-operated home for delinquent and homeless children.

The home was the material and moral center of Gilded-Age culture. St. Louisans at every economic and social level focused much of their energy on furnishing and maintaining their households. The homes that appear on every page of *Pictorial St. Louis* were the outward signs of their success; the inner workings of private life remained hidden behind dwelling walls, safe from public view.

32. Above: In Gilded-Age St. Louis, an impressive hall tree, sometimes made of cast iron, marked the dividing line between public urban space and private domestic space.

City Life

Tall spires and chimneys pierce the sky. Away off in the distance a world of green is seen where the parks [are] located, and above all rises the shriek of the whistle, the pound of the hammer, the clang of the bell, the rumble of the wagon, and the hum of thousands bent on business or pleasure.

—*Pen and Sunlight Sketches of St. Louis*, 1891

The people of Gilded-Age St. Louis differed in most of the ways that people can, but they thought of themselves collectively as St. Louisans. Shared space, common needs, and mutual dependence drew individuals into groups and groups into the larger community. A sense of communal identity did not, however, homogenize the social differences and cultural distinctions that divided local residents, especially by race, class, ethnicity, religion, age, and gender. Though variety energized urban culture, it complicated city life.

Throughout the United States, voluntary associations had long been the focus of organizational life. Like-minded people joined together to share interests, to advance causes, to be with their own, to exclude outsiders. The problems and confusions of urban life generated more voluntary groups and intensified the urge to join.

Male fraternal organizations multiplied rapidly in Gilded-Age St. Louis. Many took their names from birds and animals, or from exotic and often contrived mythologies. Stressing mystic rituals and elaborate hierarchies, these groups offered opportunities for male fellowship, the excitement of shared secrets, and social recognition outside the workplace. Most of the city's four hundred fraternal organizations selected their members on the basis of wealth, religion, race, or ethnicity. The 1880 *Gould's St. Louis Directory* listed forty-one Masonic organizations alone, including the Prince Hall Lodge for African Americans. The most exclusive local lodge was the Mystic Order of the Veiled Prophet of the Enchanted Realm, founded in 1878 to promote civic progress and define the inner circle of the business elite.

The majority of Gilded-Age fraternal organizations, however, were as much mutual-benefit insurance societies as social clubs. The Supreme Lodge Bohemian Slovenian

34. Left: Members of the Veiled Prophet organization received this banner with their invitations to the 1882 annual ball. It proclaimed the year's parade theme, "The Veiled Prophet Travels Around the World."

Benevolent Association and similar self-help societies provided disability and death benefits for workers who typically had no other insurance coverage, even though they labored under increasingly hazardous industrial conditions.

The rising tide of European immigration had a powerful effect on local organizational life. St. Louis had dozens of German social clubs, or *vereine*, because

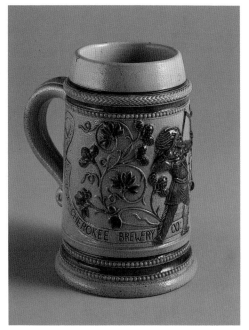

German immigrants and their children made up the largest group of ethnic St. Louisans. Local Germans were as diverse as the dozens of German principalities from which they came; many shared little beyond their ancestral language and puzzlement over American ways. German St. Louisans kept their music alive in singing societies, or *Sangervereine*, divided into at least thirty-two different groups to accommodate their members' differences in class, gender, place of origin, and musical taste. Liberal and left-wing Germans mixed politics with physical fitness in *Turnvereine* and championed religious skepticism in a free-thinkers' union, or *Freie Gemeinde*. Artists organized a *Kunstverein*, meatcutters a *Butcher-Verein*. Practically everybody joined in neighborhood beer garden fellowship.

Within their own communities, St. Louis Germans savored their differences as much as their similarities. To outsiders, however, they seemed to present a much more united front. During the Gilded Age, old-stock Americans felt increasingly threatened by immigrant newcomers. Patriotic societies promoting the national Anglo-American heritage flourished during the centennial decade of the 1870s. Ironically, the mid-1880s witnessed the dedication of the Statue of Liberty, the rise of Jim Crow, and the founding of nativist hate-groups. Historical societies organized to preserve local lore and to commemorate English—and occasionally French or Spanish—founding fathers. In 1866 descendants of St. Louis' first families established the Missouri Historical Society to preserve local relics and claim the history of the city as their own before it was too late.

The spirit of national reconciliation fostered by Civil War memorial societies also had xenophobic undertones. During the Gilded Age, St. Louisans erected public monuments to heroes both blue and gray but none to

35. Above: The Cherokee Brewery had a neighborhood beer garden at Cherokee and Iowa streets and a popular saloon at 4th and Chestnut streets.

36. Left: Ceremonial dress and rituals were important aspects of fraternal life for *Freie Gemeinde* members, some of whom had fought in the failed 1848 German revolution before immigrating to St. Louis.

Dred Scott, the most famous local African American. As Union and Confederate veterans met in St. Louis and elsewhere to commemorate the fallen, the war took on a new meaning—manly courage and shared sacrifice in the pursuit of a noble cause. By the late 1880s, nostalgia for camp life and battlefield glories had blunted once-irrepressible conflicts over labor and race. Old soldiers' encampments and Memorial Day parades smoothed the road to reunion by shunting aside concerns about the fate of former slaves.

Women—particularly those upper-class women who had done volunteer relief work for the St. Louis-based Western Sanitary Commission—tended to draw different lessons from their Civil War experience. The wartime emergency had created opportunities for charitable, educational, and administrative work that went far beyond the traditional female roles. For these women, the war had been a liberating experience that added personal dimensions to the social idealism of the Thirteenth, Fourteenth, and Fifteenth amendments. Veterans of women's Civil War relief agencies were the vanguard of post-war female activism in poor relief, educational reform, and temperance, and led the campaigns for women's suffrage and equal rights.

If shared interests bound St. Louisans together in voluntary associations, shared space bound them together in neighborhoods. Gilded-Age St. Louis had no long-lasting, discrete ethnic enclaves, however; any single working-class block might be home to people of German, Irish, English, and African descent. African Americans, who made up 6 percent of the population in 1880, lived in every city ward. Income more than race determined residential patterns.

The dozens of church spires rising above the local skyline were visible proof that people who shared the

same neighborhoods did not necessarily share the same faiths or traditions. For believers, worship was only one aspect of a church-centered family life that included schooling, social activities, and the rituals associated with birth, marriage, and death. Their choice of religious affiliation often depended as much on distinctions of race, class, and ethnicity as it did on fine points of doctrine. Nearly every Protestant denomination had a following. Separate Catholic churches, both Roman and Eastern rite, served Irish, German, Anglo-American, African-American,

37. Above: St. Louis African Americans organized the Colored Relief Board in 1879 to assist Exodusters, black refugees from the South stranded in the city on their way to Kansas.

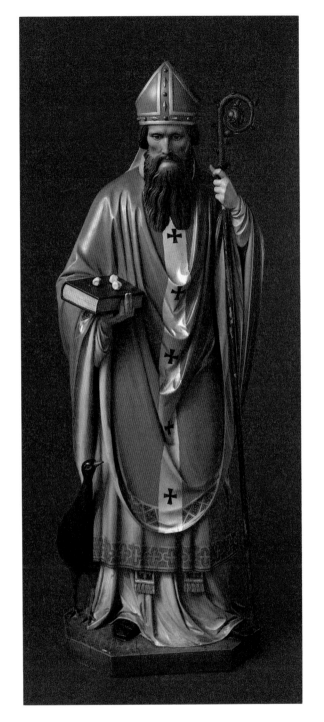

38. Left: This painted wood statue of St. Liborius stood at the entry of the elaborate St. Liborius German Catholic Church constructed in 1880 on North 18th Street.

39. Above: This sewing circle met regularly in members' homes. The photograph was a surprise gift for the woman in the center. Her friends glued an image of her head over that of the stand-in who had posed in her place.

Bohemian, Polish, Italian, and other ethnic parishioners. Clustered in a poor North Side neighborhood near Biddle Street were the first local African-American Presbyterian church; two Irish Catholic churches; German Catholic, Baptist, and Evangelical congregations; and a Jewish synagogue.

In addition to a rich array of religious organizations, Gilded-Age St. Louis offered its residents an endless variety of leisure-time activities—though work weeks of six twelve-hour days left little time or energy for fun. Most often, Gilded-Age leisure involved relaxing with family or friends close to home. Community-wide entertainments included major seasonal festivals such as the annual Agricultural and Mechanical Fair, the

Exposition, and the Veiled Prophet parade. Different theatrical performances, concerts, and lectures were available almost every day of the year, and evening diversions catered to every taste and budget.

St. Louisans could swim and ice skate indoors or out, play tennis, row, and ride. They could stroll in Henry Shaw's botanical garden or explore the new city parks on the western outskirts beyond Grand Avenue. Originally, Forest Park had been planned as a rural retreat for the urban masses, a morally uplifting alternative to the dingy streets of factory districts. Until streetcars made it easily accessible late in the Gilded Age, however, Forest Park remained the neighborhood park for the West End elite, complete with gracefully winding carriageways and a gentlemen's racetrack. In the meantime, vacant tracts within the city limits, many still wooded and dotted with ponds, provided free open space for hunting and fishing, picnics and children's play.

Among Gilded-Age sports fans, baseball was all the rage. A characteristically urban spectator sport, baseball rose with the industrial city and depended on local sponsors and enthusiastic fans to crowd the bleachers. Baseball came to St. Louis in the 1850s, and by 1874 there were five whites-only teams: the Elephants, the Empires, the St. Louis Red Stockings, the Unions, and the Stocks. The Red Stockings Baseball Park, located at Market and Compton, was the scene of amateur, semi-pro, and professional games until 1898. The St. Louis Brown Stockings, organized in 1875 as part of the National Association, was the first professional team in the city. The Browns joined the National League in 1876 and won four national championships in the 1880s playing at Sportsman's Park on Grand Avenue. The segregated Black Sox, the Eclipse, and other St. Louis African-American baseball clubs played only against each other.

Bicycling and photography became immensely popular pastimes in the late Gilded Age, in part because they appealed to men and women alike. Modern safety bicycles, so called because they were less dangerous than the poorly braked, unstable high-wheelers, appeared in the late 1880s and made cycling an appropriate female activity—although conservative critics warned that free-wheeling women posed a threat to public morality and civil order.

Another technological innovation of the 1880s—George Eastman's portable, easy-to-use Kodak snapshot camera—converted photography from a professional pursuit into a popular hobby for women as well as men. Playing to the expansive mood of the early '90s, Eastman's advertising often featured the independent, self-assured "New Woman," sometimes standing beside her bicycle with a special cyclist's Kodak mounted on the handlebars.

Lives collided daily in a crowded city, where almost every private act had a potentially public aspect. Depending on individual moods and social circumstances, the closeness of urban living could enrich or impoverish, build tolerance or breed contempt. By and large, Gilded-Age St. Louisans did their best to get along, and in their collective effort they built a diverse urban culture rich with possibilities and surprises.

40. Above: Charles Comiskey, who played on the St. Louis Browns' 1886 championship team, appeared on this early baseball card. The 1.5-by-2.5-inch card was distributed as a premium in packs of Old Judge cigarettes.

41. Left: Urban industrialism made some St. Louisans rich as it transformed the St. Louis economy, but workers like these at the Platt and Thornburgh Paint and Glass Company received little of the wealth they produced. Manufacturing workers in 1890 spent fully half their income on food.

Looking Backward

What solution, if any, have you found for the labor question? It was the Sphinx's riddle of the nineteenth century, and when I dropped out the Sphinx was threatening to devour society, because the answer was not forthcoming.

—Edward Bellamy, *Looking Backward*, 1888

42. Left: The unequal distribution of Gilded-Age wealth persisted into the 20th century, perpetuating conditions shown in this 1908 photograph of a yard on North 8th Street.

Edward Bellamy's best-selling novel, *Looking Backward*, told the story of a Bostonian who fell asleep in 1887 and awoke in the year 2000 to find himself in a tranquil, park-like city where there was full employment and social harmony, and where everyone enjoyed the material benefits of a consumer society. The popularity of *Looking Backward* was a telling measure of Gilded-Age discontent. If readers had been satisfied with the achievements of industrial capitalism, they would not have found Bellamy's totalitarian, socialist utopia so appealing. They saw *Looking Backward* as a beacon to a better way, all the more promising for its radical vision.

By the early '90s, signs of social stress and rising voices of social protest were evident in every major American city. Labor unrest, anti-immigrant agitation, and Jim Crow racism were endemic; populist protest threatened politics-as-usual. Poverty shadowed progress, and social injustice eluded reform. The best-selling social commentaries of the day—Henry George's *Progress and Poverty*, Josiah Strong's *Our Country: Its Present Perils and Future Promise,* and Bellamy's *Looking Backward*—all thoughtfully reassessed the price of progress in the Gilded Age.

Looking backward today from the 1990s, we have the historical perspective that Edward Bellamy could only imagine and had to cast in fictional form. We can assess the long-term consequences, the costs and benefits, of decisions made or avoided in Bellamy's day. We can judge for ourselves how much of the Gilded-Age legacy is a heritage to treasure and how much is a burden to overcome.

Gilded-Age St. Louisans believed that the most difficult problems facing their city and the nation were, as they termed them, "The Labor Question," "The Woman Question," and "The Negro Question." Their list, though correct as far as it went, would have been more complete if they had also perceived the long-term problems of municipal governance and environmental quality.

Workers were restive in the Gilded Age because they realized that they produced much more wealth than they enjoyed. They did not willingly or easily adapt to the conditions of dependency imposed by low wages, hard times, and poor working conditions. But for the most part workers did adapt, and their accommodations underwrote the fortunes of the mercantile and industrial elite.

In 1875 the United States Supreme Court ruled in a St. Louis case that the Fourteenth Amendment had made women citizens but not voters. Virginia Minor's failure to win women's suffrage in *Minor v. Happensett* symbolized the status of women in Gilded-Age St. Louis: free enough to demand their rights, but not yet strong enough to take them. Few local women were political or social activists, and few of their campaigns made significant headway against the inertia of masculine power.

Emancipation celebrations were hardly over before local African Americans realized that the end of slavery was not necessarily the beginning of equality. Throughout the Gilded Age, black St. Louisans continually pressed the white community for better schools and greater access to jobs with a future, but residential and social segregation continued and even increased. African Americans were not the only targets of ethnic ridicule and stereotyping in the Gilded Age. Nativists vilified Germans, the Irish, southern and eastern Europeans generally, and anyone else who seemed alien. Immigrants also brought Old World ethnic antagonisms with them to the New World, where living in crowded, ethnically mixed neighborhoods intensified conflict. But the legacy of slavery meant that only racial discrimination became institutionalized and

locked into law. The Gilded Age began hopefully with the Thirteenth Amendment; it ended with Supreme Court-sanctioned segregation.

Late nineteenth-century St. Louisans addressed the problems of economic and social injustice but found no easy solutions. At the same time, they began to confront other serious issues—notably local governance and environmental health—which were directly related to the rapid development of the industrial city.

Growth outpaced governance in Gilded-Age St. Louis. Municipal government strove to be both honest and responsive, efficient and humane, but in the daily life of a growing city these were often incompatible goals. Though residents constantly demanded more services, they balked at higher taxes. Everyone, from precinct leaders to the mayor, scrambled for political advantage, often losing sight of larger community interests in pursuit of their own. No one could agree on the best balance between public responsibility and private initiative. The 1876 divorce of St. Louis City from St. Louis County, which seemed the right thing at the time, turned out to be the wrong thing in the long run. Already river-bound on the east, now charter-bound on the west, St. Louis found itself politically isolated in the midst of its own greater metropolis.

43. Above Left: Much of the beauty of this engraving of St. Louis in 1876 came from the pall of coal smoke that enveloped the city.

44, 45. Left: Common household items, such as these cast-iron banks, often incorporated and reinforced racial and ethnic stereotypes.

46. Left: In the 1870s a political cartoonist saw graft, corruption, and impassable streets as "too much slush" in St. Louis municipal government.

Municipal politics responded best to immediate and obvious crises, but environmental damage was often subtle and took years to show its effects. The social turmoil and political disorder of Gilded-Age St. Louis made it difficult for citizens and civic leaders alike to recognize that short-term growth favoring a few might have disastrous long-term consequences for the many. What was good for business was not necessarily good for the community. Unplanned, uneven development was hard to manage and still harder to sustain. Suburban expansion left behind a collapsing core, eventually borne down by the debris of civic progress. The wealthy moved ever farther west, adding spatial distance to the social distance that separated them from the less-fortunate St. Louisans they had left behind. Even the shared problems of muddy drinking water, sooty air, and industrial pollution remained beyond collective solution.

If greatness was measured by size, wealth, influence, or grandeur, Gilded-Age St. Louis never became the fabled Future Great City of the World. Its accomplishments were more modest, though no less real or historically revealing: for the city that took shape during the Gilded Age was the foundation of the St. Louis we live in today. Traces of those foundations still surround us—visible in landscapes, artifacts, institutions, laws, habits, and memories—to remind us of our origins and hint at our destiny.

LOOKING BACKWARD

47. Right: North Grand
Avenue water tower from the
west, 1993

Perspectives

SAINT LOUIS IN THE GILDED AGE

Pictorial St. Louis: A Topographical Survey Drawn in Perspective A.D. 1875 is the most detailed bird's-eye view of an American city ever published. It portrays every street and structure at this defining moment in the late nineteenth century, when the city was evolving from a frontier trading center into a modern industrial metropolis. No other single artifact of Gilded-Age St. Louis so well conveys the character of the place or the spirit of the times.

Like other landscapes, cityscapes show the topography of time. Traces of the past accumulate like geological strata, with some layers clearly exposed and others partially hidden or obscured by subsequent events. *Pictorial St. Louis* is a map of the historical terrain, a volume of visual facts and intriguing clues that hint at what the city had been, what it was like in 1875, and what it might become.

Today, the area shown on Plate 45 seems little more than an urban wasteland cut through by Interstate 70, yet the aged buildings and the street names recall a rich past. Mound Street commemorates the huge Native American earthworks that once dominated the St. Louis skyline. The bends in Broadway and the numbered streets still mark the collision points between eighteenth-century French land grants and nineteenth-century Yankee surveys.

The thriving urban scene of 1875 is long gone, but Camille Dry's sketches remain to give us a glimpse of what it was like: a densely populated walking city of pedestrians and horse-drawn streetcars where stores and factories shared blocks with close-packed row houses, freestanding homes, and public buildings. In 1875, workers converted logs into lumber at the Empire Mill Company (#18) and the Pacific Planing Mill (#20). They made cast-iron stoves at the St. Louis Stove Works (#19) and manufactured carriages (#12) and chairs (#15). Their families shopped at the Mound Market (#11), banked at the Mullanphy Savings Bank (#10), and worshiped at the North St. Louis Christian Church (#16) or at other neighborhood Roman Catholic and Protestant churches. Some of their children attended the nearby Webster Public School. Firemen from the Mound Fire Company (#13) protected their homes. Residents doubtless knew the now long-forgotten function of the large-wheeled carts parked on the vacant lot on 9th Street.

For all their engrossing detail, Camille Dry's static scenes show forms better than functions. They only suggest the bustle of movement and process under way in the streets and behind the walls. Like a traveler's guide to a foreign country, *Pictorial St. Louis* offers a taste of the exotic. Every page is both a revelation and a mystery—an invitation to explore.

48. Facing: Detail, Plate 45, *Pictorial St. Louis*

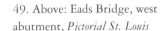

49. Above: Eads Bridge, west abutment, *Pictorial St. Louis*

50. Left: Eads Bridge, 1874

More Than Meets the Eye

A bird's-eye view is a kind of map, and every map distorts geographical reality in order to reveal it. Mapmakers shrink the terrain to a convenient scale and project it on a flat plane, thus warping the curved surface of the earth. They de-emphasize or ignore some features in order to highlight others; they select and interpret, tailoring distortions and omissions to the particular purposes at hand. Any map is only one of many possible images of the same geographic area. Each one is a coded text, an artifact of time and place, motive and method, fact and fantasy.

Pictorial St. Louis is a book of bird's-eye views conceived as a profitable and flattering urban portrait, the graphic centerpiece of a civic crusade promoting St. Louis as "The Future Great City of the World." Instead of the usual long-range, bird's-eye urban overview printed on a single sheet, *Pictorial St. Louis* is a bound volume of 110 intricately detailed lithographic plates, reinforced by booster text. It renders St. Louis as an aggregation of private parcels and individual enterprises, a civic celebration of Gilded-Age self-made manhood and family accomplishment. The book sold only by pre-publication subscription at $25 a copy (or about $325 in current dollars). In the midst of a crushing depression, it was an extravagant purchase for all but the wealthy. *Pictorial St. Louis* proved to be a commercial flop, but it remains an artistic triumph and a historical puzzle with hidden meanings that await discovery on every page.

The almost photographic realism of *Pictorial St. Louis* disarms the viewer with its seeming truth. Other, more heavy-handed Gilded-Age booster maps gave themselves away, as did the 1874 *Central Magazine* cover that showed "The Future Great City" much larger than life and set against a background shaded in concentric circles to emphasize the city's central position as a national transportation hub (53).

The more subtle distortions and omissions of *Pictorial St. Louis* easily escape notice. Despite James Eads' hand-written endorsement, the *Pictorial St. Louis* frontispiece view of heroic statuary on Eads Bridge is a visual lie (49). The statues were planned but never installed, yet they appeared in all early and most later graphic views and fixed themselves in the public mind. Contemporaries apparently overlooked the contradiction between what they saw in life and what they saw in print. Later generations, ignoring the absence of statuary in all Eads Bridge photographs, puzzled fruitlessly over what had happened to things that had never been (50).

Contemporary photographs often help to flesh out Camille Dry's bare-bones bird's-eye views, as in the case of this 1874 image of Main Street north of Walnut Street (51, 52). The camera captures many of the gritty realities of Gilded-Age street life missing from the draftsman's sketch. Yet photographs, like maps, portraits, and other shadows of the visual past, finally reveal only what beholders are prepared to see. Viewed uncritically, they often show more—and sometimes less—than first meets the eye.

51. Left: Walnut and Main streets, *Pictorial St. Louis*

52. Below Left: Main Street north from Walnut Street, 1874

53. Below: *Central Magazine* cover, 1874

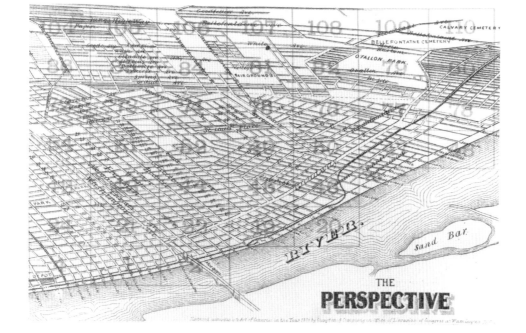

THE
PERSPECTIVE

54. Above: Key to *Pictorial St. Louis* plates, northern part of city

55. Right: Currier and Ives view of St. Louis, northern part of city

Cityscapes

There is no ideal way to portray a cityscape. Low-angle views in the manner of conventional landscape paintings show foreground features, but they hide background details and the pattern of the streets. Map-like overhead views reveal the street layout but little else. Views parallel to any street axis show only facing facades.

During the Gilded Age, urban viewmakers usually resorted to a graphic compromise. On a single sheet, they drew an overview of a whole city in one- or two-point perspective from an imaginary, elevated vantage point at an angle to the main street axis. Such a "bird's-eye" view showed topography, the street patterns, building elevations, and something of the character of the community—at least in the foreground. Background details dissolved in a blur, however, as buildings shrank and lines converged toward the vanishing point. An otherwise-elegant 1874 Currier and Ives view of St. Louis illustrates these inherent limitations of conventional bird's-eye perspective (55).

Pictorial St. Louis presented a radically different view of the cityscape. A multiplate mosaic rather than a single sheet, it utilized a peculiar perspective that enabled Camille Dry to render every St. Louis street and structure with equal clarity. Dry was the only American viewmaker to attempt such a technical and artistic feat, and the only viewmaker to explain his graphic method.

As Dry described his technique, he first imagined how the city would look to a viewer high above the Mississippi River. From that vantage point he drew a perspective overview of the city, divided it into 110 numbered

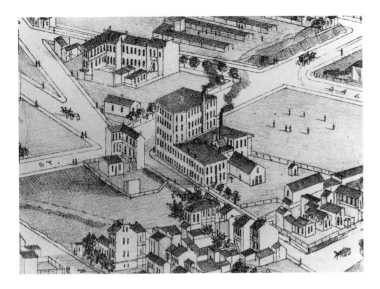

sections, and prepared a detailed drawing of each section as a separate sheet. His overview, "Key to the Perspective," shows how the individual sections aligned and how the Key served as a locator index (54).

The artist actually misrepresented what he had done. Both the Key and its text implied some kind of fixed-point perspective, but such a view would have produced all the usual problems of foreshortening and convergence. Dry actually shifted his vantage point from plate to plate in order to picture each section of the city from a roughly constant distance, elevation, and compass bearing.

The resulting views were more like modern zoom-lens aerial panoramas than traditional bird's-eye views. No other viewmaker came close to portraying a whole city with such consistently intimate and seemingly three-dimensional realism. The spires of the Centenary Methodist Episcopal and First Christian churches are barely discernible in the center right area of the Currier and Ives view, but they appear sharply delineated in *Pictorial St. Louis* (57). Far-distant Natural Bridge Road

was little more than a line near the horizon on the one, a suburban neighborhood on the other (56).

Camille Dry's graphic tricks revealed some characteristics of Gilded-Age St. Louis, but they obscured others. In an era of widening social distinctions and spatial separations, he was remarkably inclusive and even-handed, sketching the precincts of both rich and poor in the same meticulous detail. Yet his division of the city into 110 sections magnified each one at the expense of the whole, and the bound-book format of *Pictorial St. Louis* made it impossible to view more than one section at a time. For all its richness of urban detail, the book provided no comprehensive perspective, no explanation of how different areas of the city related to each other, no sense that a city is more than the sum of its parts.

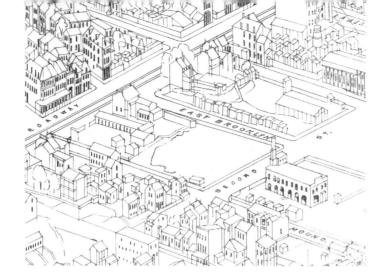

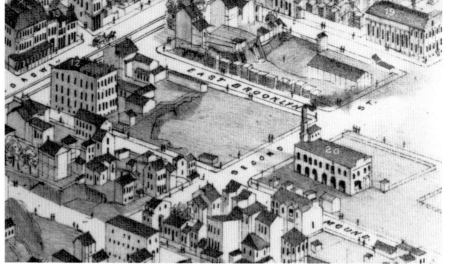

Democratic Vistas

Pictorial St. Louis is an album of drawings, not snapshots. Even though Camille Dry and his assistants often achieved near-photographic accuracy, there was considerable room for artistic license as they painstakingly redrew each image: first as a rough field sketch; then as a studio line drawing in perspective; next as a shaded, finished rendering; and finally as a reversed image on the stone lithographic plate used to print the published view.

At every stage the viewmakers had to make choices, balancing their own artistry against their patron's preferences and the dictates of graphic necessity. They could show outsides of buildings but not insides, public activity but not private life, tangible products but not fleeting processes. They often sketched in nonexistent thoroughfares, and they chose to picture a completed

Post Office and Customs House, which was really only half-built. The streets of *Pictorial St. Louis* appear clean, tidy, and nearly deserted, when in reality they were dirty, crowded, and alive with people and animals.

A preliminary sketch, compared with the final drawing, offers clues to the technique the artists employed (58, 59). At first glance the two views appear the same except for the all-important shading, which clarifies details and adds to the illusion of depth. However, a closer look reveals subtle though important differences, such as the large carriage factory at Broadway and Mound which is prominent in the final view but missing entirely from the line drawing. At the same time, the final view includes a few direct signs of life—pedestrians, passing vehicles, smoke from working factories—while the preliminary sketch shows an apparently deserted city.

Camille Dry's lithographs have an almost abstract quality compared to the immediacy of contemporary photographs. A photograph of McCreery's Livery and Boarding Stables at 9th and Pine, taken after 1875, brings to life a street corner that is lost and lifeless in

Pictorial St. Louis (61). Looming behind the livery stable is the rising superstructure of the new federal Custom House and Post Office; it is shown here in another photograph as it actually looked when Dry drew it (62). The school visible behind the construction site also appears in *Pictorial St. Louis* (60).

Modern viewers can tease a great deal from historical images, but they cannot see things that are not there. What is missing from *Pictorial St. Louis* are democratic vistas of St. Louisans at work, at home, at play, caught up together in the swirl of urban living. In part by necessity, in part by design, *Pictorial St. Louis* is a better portrait of property than people.

60. Above Right: Custom House and Post Office and surrounding neighborhood, *Pictorial St. Louis*

61. Below: The livery stable at 9th and Pine streets, c.1880

62. Above: Custom House and Post Office under construction, November 7, 1875

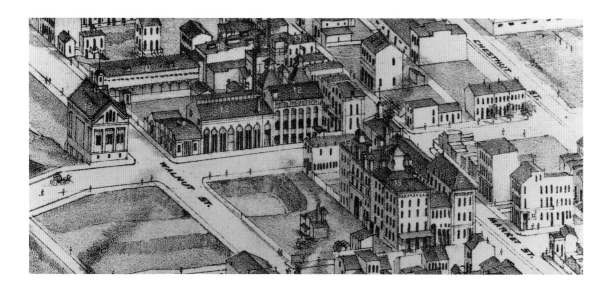

Layers of Time

For all its limitations, *Pictorial St. Louis* is a valuable historical source, a tour guide to a lost urban world. Frozen in time, Camille Dry's careful renderings of particular places in 1875 serve as graphic points of reference for later views of the same scenes. Just as geological strata record the natural history of the earth, dated drawings and photographs document the sequence of human occupancy and use. The visual record of a particular urban site also provides indirect evidence for the evolution of the city as a whole.

In 1875, the area between Market and Walnut west of 18th Street (63) was far from the central business district; it was a fringe area cluttered with a jumble of horse stables, a wagon factory, and the buildings of Uhrig's Brewery. South of Walnut Street, the land sloped away to the broad valley that had held Chouteau's Pond before it was drained in the 1850s. Now, the former pond site was a busy rail yard filled with tracks, switches, and sidings.

In 1894, the same area, by then on the western edge of the central business district, became the site of the magnificent new Union Station designed by Theodore Link. Each day a thousand passenger cars passed through its ten-acre, vaulted train shed that stretched southward behind the monumental Market Street facade (64). By the turn of the century, Union Station had become the main gateway to the city. All rail travelers arriving from east or west changed trains there. The station and its immediate surroundings were all of St. Louis many visitors ever saw.

Union Station was not unique; during the nineteenth century every major American city built an imposing railway terminal which was, more often than not,

63. Top: Site of Union Station as it appeared in 1875, *Pictorial St. Louis*

64. Above: Union Station train shed, 1907

Union Station, ST. LOUIS, U. S. A.

reminiscent of medieval architecture. The fortress-like stone structure incorporated several traditional motifs: a tall watchtower, large stained-glass windows, vaulted ceilings, Romanesque arches, and a Spanish tile roof. Widely pictured in romanticized postcard views, Union Station served local boosters well as a dual symbol of tradition and modernity, a secular church dedicated to steam and steel (65).

The vast midway separating the train shed from the depot teemed with passengers until after World War II, when rail travel gave way to automobiles and commercial airliners (66). In the post-war years, Lambert Field and interstate highway bridges became the gateways to St. Louis. The last train left Union Station in 1978.

For more than a decade, the derelict station and its surrounding area remained in limbo while St. Louisans debated the function and future of their declining downtown. During the 1980s, Union Station revived in the enthusiasm of urban renewal, not as a transportation hub but as a shopping mall and convention center—the latest layer in the material strata of time (67).

Landscapes

SAINT LOUIS IN THE GILDED AGE

Because every event has a place as well as a time, locale frames historical experience. Particular places take on particular meanings as each generation organizes space and commits land to use. Landscape reflects values and priorities, gives tangible form to the social order, and marks change over time. Geography nails history to the ground.

All urban landscapes are similar in that cities are, by definition, relatively large, densely populated, and complex. Each community, however, has its own special location, climate, topography, demography, form, function, and feel. The distinctive geography of a place, no less than the spirit of its times, shapes its historical possibilities and offers evidence of how things come to be.

The rail yards, abandoned truck terminals, and derelict factories that today line Chouteau Avenue between Grand and Vandeventer avenues give little indication of the area's earlier history. *Pictorial St. Louis* is more revealing, because Camille Dry's bird's-eye view of the area in 1875 highlights some of the geographic elements—the lay of the land, a large spring, a major thoroughfare, and a nearby railroad—that explain its evolution from countryside to cityscape.

In the early nineteenth century, the area had been the main settlement in Rock Spring Township, a rustic retreat of springs, ponds, and picturesque country houses. Well-traveled Manchester Road provided easy access from the city. Businesses and residences clustered along this section of Manchester (now Chouteau) near the Rock Spring Hotel (#3), a popular country inn.

Rock Spring itself was the principal source of Mill Creek, which flowed eastward through the valley between Market and Chouteau streets. Early settlers had dammed the creek for a mill pond (Chouteau's Pond), incidentally forming the physical barrier that was to separate South St. Louis from the rest of the community. When St. Louisans drained the pond in the 1850s, Mill Creek Valley became the route of the Pacific Railroad, visible in the lower

left corner of the plate. Pacific promoters incorporated the town of Rock Spring in 1852.

By the early 1870s, a tannery (#4), a bone-black factory (#5), and a varnish works (#6) had brought industrial jobs, more people, and noisome pollution to the area, even though Camille Dry portrayed it still surrounded by bucolic countryside. In later years, further industrial expansion wiped out all vestiges of the original rural landscape. Rock Spring and Mill Creek disappeared from view into underground sewers, their physical presence commemorated only in historic place-names.

Rock Spring illustrates the historical geography of a specific locale and points to the larger significance of place in St. Louis history. Indeed, St. Louisans have always been conscious of place and have understood their history in terms of two broadly geographic concepts, the first founded on hope, the second rooted in experience. They long fancied that their city would be borne forward by superhuman forces of geographical destiny. According to the local founding myth, retold on the opening page of *Pictorial St. Louis*, the city's founding fathers had known in 1763 that St. Louis would one day be the great metropolis of the mid-Mississippi Valley. In 1849 local promoters launched the first transcontinental railroad because they believed that it would funnel the riches of Asia through St. Louis. The same kind of faith in cosmic laws of latitude fed booster dreams of civic greatness throughout the Gilded Age and well into the twentieth century.

St. Louisans' second geographical idea was far more down to earth, rooted in the realities of landscape and accumulated historical experience. Local geography, like local history, played favorites in response to growing diversity. While the fortunate strove to reshape Gilded-Age St. Louis in the image of their dreams, other residents less advantaged by timing, talent, wealth, or luck made the best of the city as they found it. Over the years, spatial divisions increasingly mirrored social distinctions. As particular places became identified with particular groups and thereby took on symbolic meanings, landscapes shaded into mindscapes.

68. Facing: Detail, Plate 87, *Pictorial St. Louis*

The Lay of the Land

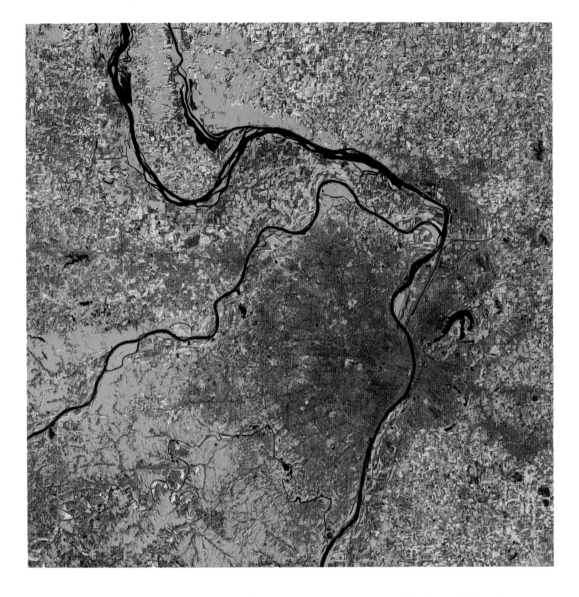

69. Above: False-color satellite image of St. Louis region, 1988

Crunching ice and falling water shaped the midwestern landscape. Over a span of some 40,000 years, advancing glaciers flattened and furrowed the land, then left new deposits behind in their retreat. Each new glacial cycle plowed and filled again. Massive run-off from the melting ice sheets collected in lakes and cut wide river valleys. After the last glaciers receded, water and wind erosion continued to reshape the land. The result was the gently rolling prairie heartland: rich-soiled, well watered, drained by the Mississippi River and its tributaries (70). Modern satellite photographs highlight the patterns etched by ice and water (69).

From its central location on the western bank of the Mississippi, above the Ohio but below the Missouri and the Illinois rivers, St. Louis was well positioned to dominate the region—as long as the rivers remained the main arteries of communication and trade.

The city's river valley topography shaped its physical form and historical development. Since St. Louis occupied the only high bank, it was unlikely that a serious rival city would ever rise on the flood plain across the river in Illinois. The sloping St. Louis shoreline provided more than a mile of levee space for docking steamboats, then rose to a low bluff that kept the city safe from floods. Behind the bluff, the prairies rolled away to the west. Though cut by numerous streams and pockmarked with sinkholes and ponds, the prairies posed no serious physical obstacle to urban growth until they fell away to the valleys of the Missouri and Meramec.

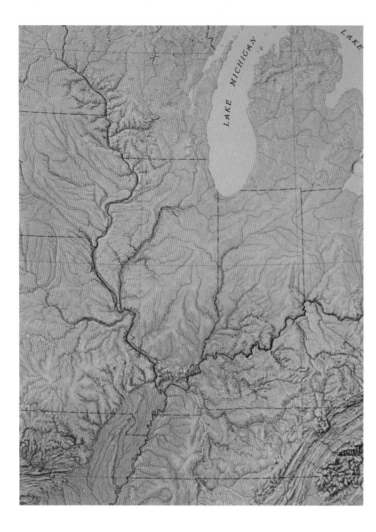

Industrializing St. Louis consumed a huge amount of energy, and like other cities, its energy options usually came down to whichever sources were most readily available at the lowest cost. The nearest, biggest, and cleanest energy source was the Mississippi River itself. The stream descended so gradually as it passed St. Louis, however, that there was no practical way to harness its enormous power. At normal river stage, a mere ten-foot falls would have provided the city with more than 260,000 horsepower—endlessly renewable and pollution-free—but St. Louis had no natural falls, and a ten-foot dam would have drowned the upstream valley far back into Iowa.

St. Louis had to rely instead on soft coal, the primary fuel of Gilded-Age industrialism. Thick coal seams underlay much of nearby southern Illinois, providing a ready supply of low-cost industrial and home-heating fuel delivered by coal boat or by rail across the Eads Bridge (71). Small-scale local miners also exploited the less-extensive coal deposits below the city itself.

Though cheap in dollars, coal was expensive in the social costs of urban grime and air pollution. Only a few Gilded-Age St. Louisans worried about such environmental drawbacks, however; most residents welcomed belching smokestacks as signs of civic progress.

Hedged by rivers on the east, north, and south, St. Louis grew into a wedge-shaped, three-sectored city that fanned out from the Mississippi. A central corridor—the historic axis of local wealth and power—extended due west from the original village site, both anchoring and separating the industrial and residential sectors on either side. North St. Louis filled in earlier and more densely than South St. Louis; indeed, much of southwest St. Louis remained relatively isolated and underdeveloped well into the twentieth century.

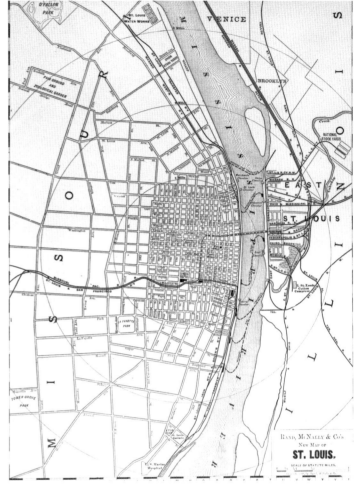

72. Above: Engraving from title page, *Pictorial St. Louis*

73. Right: Map of St. Louis rail connections, 1888

Metropolis of the Mississippi Valley

The full force and reach of the Mississippi were hard to comprehend. By the time the river reached St. Louis, twelve hundred miles below its source in a small Minnesota lake, it carried the run-off from a drainage basin that extended north to the Canadian border, east into Indiana, and west to the Rockies. At normal river stage, 240,000 cubic feet of water swirled past St. Louis every second. More tributaries poured in below St. Louis; from source to delta, the Mississippi drained more than a million square miles.

The river was many things: a seemingly living organism, powerful, willful, beautiful, seductive, and dangerous; a commercial waterway and yet a bar to overland trade; a pervasive natural presence that gave river towns their distinctive character.

The Mississippi influenced every aspect of local life. Even after the rise of railroads during the Gilded Age, the river remained vital to the economy and continued to influence how local residents saw themselves and related to their surroundings.

On the title page of *Pictorial St. Louis*, the Mississippi appears even larger than life (72). Its broad expanse more

than fills the foreground; the accentuated perspective makes it look like an endless highway, busy with trade and spanned by a bridge that links the communities on either bank. Few other views have ever pictured the metropolis in this way because St. Louis has remained a stubbornly one-sided city with a westward orientation and an odd ambivalence toward the river.

The Mississippi, though always majestic and often profitable, was rarely friendly. Swift currents and heavy commercial traffic made it a dangerous place to play. Gilded-Age St. Louisans built no riverfront parks, and the local elite preferred the flat prairies of Lucas Place and Lafayette Park to the panoramic vistas of river-bluff building sites on South Broadway.

In 1874, the Eads Bridge linked St. Louis not only to the national rail network but also to the eastern half of its expanding metropolitan hinterland (73). This decisive change in spatial economics had little direct effect on local spatial consciousness. The river remained a mental boundary. East St. Louis remained a place apart, generally out of sight and out of mind.

The driving forces of Gilded-Age St. Louis all converged at the western approach to the Eads Bridge, where river and rail met commerce and community (74). This section of the levee was perhaps the most dynamic place in the city. While boats maneuvered and draymen loaded cargo, ferry passengers filed up the levee, across the railroad tracks, and onto Washington Avenue. Overhead, trains and vehicles rumbled across the double-decked bridge. Even Camille Dry's still-life sketch conveys a sense of movement and change in this fluid zone of arrivals, departures, and possibilities. Dry shows the old Wiggins Ferry still in operation but now in the shadow of the new Eads Bridge; from their office at the corner of Vine Street, ferry operators could witness the slow collapse of their former river-crossing monopoly.

The same scene, photographed at midday from the top of the west abutment, confirms the overall accuracy of Camille Dry's lithograph but fills in the scene with more life-like riverfront dirt and clutter (75). The photographer probably shot the strangely vacant levee scene on a Sunday morning, when businesses were closed and workers at home. A Gilded-Age camera would have pictured the bustle of normal weekday activity as a meaningless blur.

74. Above Left: St. Louis levee, *Pictorial St. Louis*

75. Above: Levee south of Eads Bridge, 1879

76. Left: Intersection of Olive and Taylor, *Pictorial St. Louis*

77. Below: Map of northern St. Louis land surveys, 1847

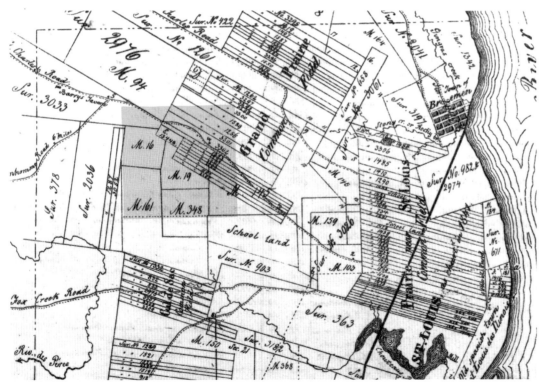

Boundaries

oundaries partition space, define land use, and proclaim ownership. They give form to community, and by limiting the range of individual action, encourage social cohesion. Boundary lines often persist long after time has erased their original logic.

The topography of St. Louis was level enough for almost any pattern of land use residents desired. The result was a patchwork city built by successive generations who had very different ideas about how St. Louis should look and work.

The eighteenth-century Creoles who first laid out the riverfront village also divided their privately owned, outlying "common fields" into narrow plots about two hundred feet wide by a mile and a half long. The long lots reflected European farming practices dating back to medieval times. Drawn as much out of habit as necessity, this traditional pattern of village house lots and surrounding fields established the legal foundations of local land ownership and thus gave the St. Louis landscape much of its distinctive character.

Later residents drew different lines on the land. Early Anglo-American settlers from the South paced off boundaries that meandered with the topography. Jeffersonian expansionists and Yankee lawyers followed with tidy rectangular surveys that all but ignored topography but were precise enough to stand up in court. Rebelling against this monotonous checkerboard grid, late nineteenth- and twentieth-century developers platted the serpentine roadways of modern suburbia. Railroads and interstate highways cut wide swaths with little regard to their impact on community life. Sometimes

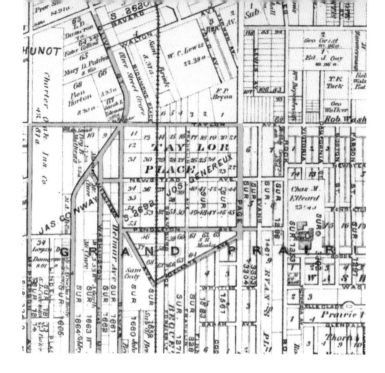

78. Far Left: Map of area surrounding Olive and Taylor, 1878

79. Left: Map of same location, 1891

deliberately but often incidentally, limited-access transportation corridors formed the boundaries of areas that residents eventually came to think of as "neighborhoods."

The area near the intersections of Washington, Delmar, and Taylor avenues and Olive Street Road, illustrates how persistent and sometimes hidden boundaries shaped the urban landscape over time. In 1875 *Pictorial St. Louis* showed the area as suburban fringe, invaded by the westward extensions of Washington and Delmar avenues (76). An earlier survey plat helped to explain the street pattern, which partially followed the old Creole boundaries of the Grand Prairie Common fields (77). The parcel labeled M. 19 identified a later American grant to Joseph Genereaux, a replacement for land he had lost to the 1811-12 New Madrid earthquakes in southeast Missouri.

Three years after Camille Dry sketched the streets for *Pictorial St. Louis*, another local mapmaker drew the same area from a realtor's perspective, showing it crisscrossed with boundary lines and subdivided into a jumble of private holdings (78). The boundaries of the Genereaux tract, now traced by Williams and Celeste avenues, collided with the rectangular grid of newly laid-out Taylor Place. The jog in Olive Street Road probably skirted around the property of some once-influential landowner.

Shifting boundaries charted the course of urban development. By the late 1890s, Olive Street Road had been realigned and Williams and Celeste avenues had disappeared. The grid prevailed as land values increased and the area filled with large brick townhouses on relatively small lots. By the 1890s, what had once been a corner of the village common fields was fast becoming the heart of the West End (79).

The Great Divide

80. Top: Mill creek sewer construction, c.1868

81. Above: Mill Creek Valley, *Pictorial St. Louis*

There were few natural barriers to impede urban growth and development as St. Louis fanned out westward from the Mississippi River. The exception was Mill Creek Valley, the great divide that separated the city—physically at first, then later socially and politically.

Mill Creek Valley had formed the southern boundary of the original village of St. Louis, and from colonial times until the 1850s it was the site of Chouteau's Pond. Needing waterpower for a grist mill, early settlers had created the pond by damming La Petite Rivière — afterwards called Mill Creek—near its mouth at the Mississippi. The mill pond filled much of the wide valley as far west as 20th Street.

Early in the nineteenth century, the pond was a source of industrial power and a favorite fishing and picnicking retreat. By the 1850s it had become a pestilential open sewer filled with foul industrial wastes. In the aftermath of the 1849 cholera epidemic, the city drained the pond and later enclosed Mill Creek in a mammoth sewer, shown under construction in a 1868 daguerreotype (80).

Draining Chouteau's Pond opened the broad, flat valley floor—now a vast, vacant tract in the midst of the city—for development, just at the time when the Pacific Railroad needed a right-of-way to the west. When railroad development revived after the Civil War, the east end of Mill Creek Valley quickly filled with train yards, then with rail-dependent factories and warehouses.

Pictorial St. Louis showed a bridge over Mill Creek Valley at 14th Street (81). Until the 1850s this crossing, plus two more at 3rd and 5th streets, had been the only

82. Far Left: Downtown
St. Louis from Benton Place,
c.1875

83. Left: Highway 40
construction, 1965

84. Below: St. Louis street
barrier, 1993

routes across the divide. Physical separation—first by Chouteau's Pond and then by the rail yards—had retarded southside development. An 1870 view of St. Louis looking to the north across the 21st Street viaduct from Benton Place conveyed the southsiders' sense of isolation from the apparently distant city (82). Few roads and little public transit then crossed the railroad tracks. Until the completion of the Grand Avenue viaduct in 1889, the southside area surrounding Tower Grove Park remained largely undeveloped because the closest crossing to downtown was nearly a mile to the east at Jefferson Avenue.

Physical isolation reinforced ethnic and class divisions between southsiders and other St. Louisans. Social and cultural differences—both real and imagined—hardened into attitudes. St. Louisans came to picture their city as divided into North St. Louis and South St. Louis: two separate places; two distinct cultures; each with a capitalized, proper name.

In the early twentieth century, African-American migrants who had recently arrived from the rural South settled on the northern edge of Mill Creek Valley near Jefferson Avenue, an area of aged housing and cheap rents. Federally funded urban renewal programs leveled their neighborhood in the 1960s. An 1965 aerial photograph showed Compton Avenue in the foreground, crossing the bulldozed landscape, and Highway 40 under construction through Mill Creek Valley (83). Market Street veered northward into the central business district.

Highway 40 became the main east-west thoroughfare connecting St. Louis to its expanding western suburbs, but its limited-access and often elevated right-of-way formed yet another great divide between North and South St. Louis. Ironically, Highway 40 also isolated county residents from urban life; they regularly traveled its secure route for business or baseball but rarely strayed far afield on unknown and unsettling surface streets.

Meanwhile, African Americans displaced by Mill Creek Valley redevelopment moved north and west, where they found boundaries drawn by race and class instead of physical geography (84).

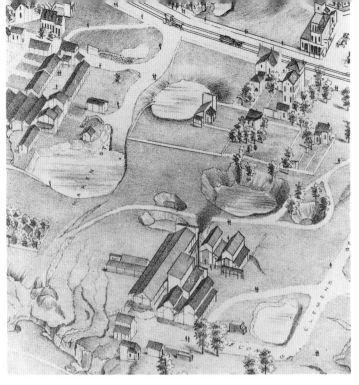

85. Above: Quarry and sinkhole, *Pictorial St. Louis*

86. Right: Oehler's Brickyard (top left) and Armstrong Press Brick Company (bottom right), *Pictorial St. Louis*

Subterranean St. Louis

Below the visible landscape lay hidden geological formations that shaped surface features and often determined what residents did with the land. Breweries located near caves and artesian springs, sometimes converting the caves into spacious beer halls as well as naturally cool aging cellars. Sinkholes and ponds influenced the character of the sewer system. Mine tailings throughout the region attested to the importance of mineral products, especially lead, iron, and clay, in the St. Louis economy.

Subterranean St. Louis had formed during the hundreds of millions of years when swamps and shallow seas covered what is now the Mississippi Valley. Transformed by heat, pressure, and time, accumulated layers of sea-bottom sediments and swampy muck had eventually hardened into the thick beds of limestone and shale, clay and coal that underlay the city. For millions of years, rainwater seeped

through cracks in the strata, riddling the limestone with caves. Collapsed cave ceilings showed on the surface as sinkholes; filled with rain water, sinkholes became ponds.

From the eighteenth century onward, workers added manmade holes and tunnels to a local landscape already honeycombed by natural forces. Gilded-Age quarrymen cut limestone building blocks from the river bluffs and sometimes from outcroppings in the midst of residential developments (85). Brickyards left a trail of abandoned clay pits, while fire-clay and coal miners left mazes of tunnels deep underground.

Until the mid-1870s, most common building bricks were still handmade in wooden molds. Master molders, like those who worked at Paul Oehler's brickyard in South St. Louis, could turn out about 3,000 bricks a day (86). Brick manufacturing changed rapidly after the 1870s with the introduction of denser, cheaper, and more uniform

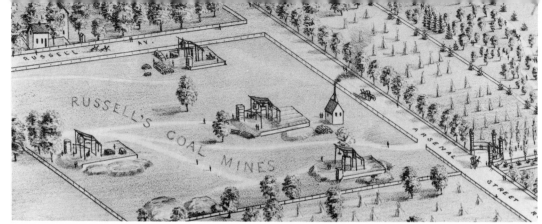

machine-made bricks, pressed in steel molds by powerful hydraulic rams. Hard, weather-resistant pressed bricks made brick street paving practical for the first time. St. Louis laid its first pressed brick streets and alleys in 1895.

The local brick industry quickly evolved from many small brickyards to a few large plants, from hand to machine technology, and from individual proprietors to large corporations. In 1875, when Camille Dry sketched Paul Oehler's traditional brickyard and the nearby Armstrong Press Brick Company, the latter was running three presses at once to fill an order for half-a-million bricks for a nearby building site. By 1891, the thirty-nine St. Louis brickyards were turning out 245 million bricks a year (87). The Hydraulic Press Brick Company, located in the River Des Peres bottoms near Manchester Road in Cheltenham, was the nation's largest supplier; its kilns burned ten freight cars of coal a day. Cheltenham decorative terra cotta and industrial fire clay products were also in high demand.

The coal seams underlying St. Louis were too scattered to warrant large-scale mining. Local coal mines, such as Russell's, across Arsenal Street from Tower Grove Park,

87. Far Left: Worker at the Progress Press Brick Company, 1890

88. Above: Russell's Coal Mine, *Pictorial St. Louis*

89. Left: Coal mining on Gravois Road, c.1855

were small diggings that supplied area residents with household fuel (88). Neighborhood coal mines were especially common in South St. Louis, where the coal often lay close to the surface and where perennially poor road conditions ran up delivery charges on small lots of coal mined elsewhere (89).

Holes in the ground are sometimes natural features and usually seem to lack historical significance. But in Gilded-Age St. Louis, holes, caves, and tunnels were often revealing historical artifacts, by-products of industry, and evidence of enterprise. These lowly and often ignored subterranean features traced the rise of the city no less than surface streets and structures.

Transformations

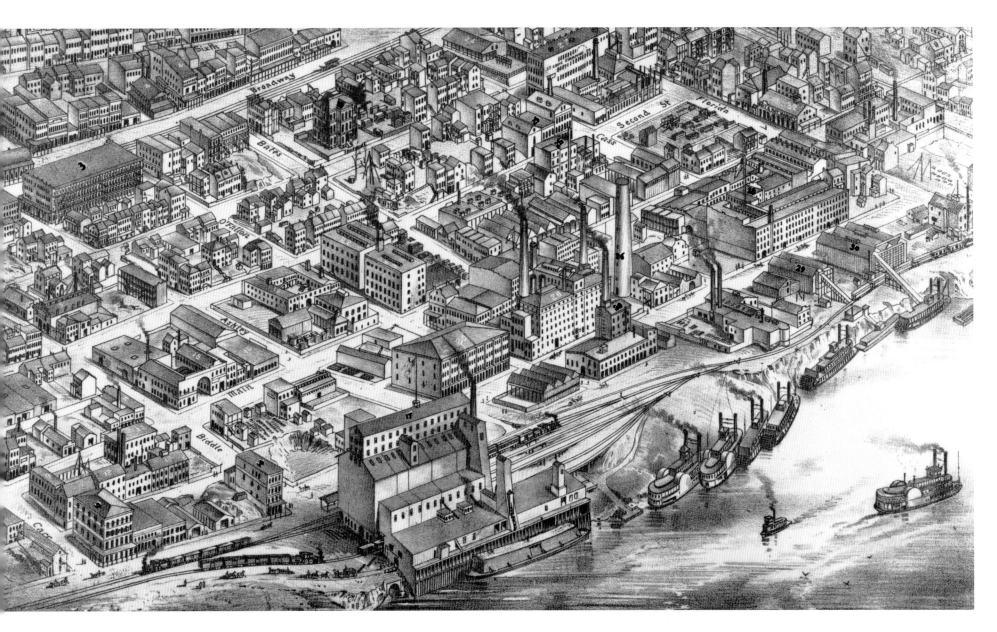

Cities bustle with ceaseless activity. Goods are created, transported, processed, transformed. People hurry about, prosper, fail, begin again. Yet little of this headlong urban rush is evident on the pages of *Pictorial St. Louis*. What appear instead are hints and shadows of change and process, clues to transformations under way on the streets and behind the walls.

One of the busiest industrial districts in Gilded-Age St. Louis was the near-northside area between Broadway and the river, Carr Street and Cass Avenue. There was a constant traffic of riverboats and barges, streetcars and trains, wagons, carriages, and pedestrians. Draymen threaded through the streets to the railroad depots between Carr and Biddle streets (#10, #14). Raw materials streamed in from distant places: Illinois River ice for local breweries (#29 and #30); Caribbean raw sugar for the Belcher Sugar Refinery (#20); Missouri lead for the St. Louis Shot Tower and a paint pigment plant (#26, #25); midwestern grain for the St. Louis Elevator (#17). Major industries clustered nearby, notably the Excelsior Stove Works, whose "Charter Oak" ranges were regional favorites (#28); the Murphy Wagon Works, home of the most popular freight wagon in the West ; the St. Louis Novelty Works, an oddly named supplier of builders' and contractors' supplies; and the St. Louis Stamping Company, makers of the popular new porcelain-glazed Granite Iron Ware cooking utensils.

The largest enterprises sprawled across whole blocks. East of the Belcher refinery, across Lewis Street, stood the refinery's bone-black mill, which purified caramelized waste into carbon. To the west across Main, the refinery's cooperage filled the block between Ashley and O'Fallon.

Signs of process and transformation filled the scene, but actual human activity was less obvious. Readers of *Pictorial St. Louis* had to imagine the thousands of workers who crowded the streets twice each day, coming and going in response to the scream of factory whistles. Images of smoking chimneys only hinted at the din of pulsating machinery and the toxic fumes that filled the air.

Yet even *Pictorial St. Louis* makes it clear that Gilded-Age St. Louisans lived in the midst of this industrial pandemonium, and that in those times of rapid industrialization lives as well as goods were being transformed. In this bustling world of precarious fortunes, everyone and everything was in flux. The presence of a public school (#23) indicated both a youthful neighborhood and a growing public concern about schooling. Area housing was crowded; turnover was high. The four square blocks between Ashley and Bates, Broadway and Second streets featured all the significant local styles: freestanding, single-family dwellings; common-wall row houses; back-alley shacks; and even a huge, multistory tenement, a Gilded-Age commonplace in eastern cities but still unusual in St. Louis (#3).

90. Facing: Detail, Plate 19, *Pictorial St. Louis*

91. Above: Passenger Station and freight depots, *Pictorial St. Louis*

Transporting

During the Gilded Age, railroad transportation tied the nation's far-flung regions into a single, interdependent economy. By reducing transportation time and cost, railroads created national markets which in turn stimulated regional specialization. Railroads were also the first modern "big business" ventures; they pioneered new forms of corporate organization and management, stimulated new industries, generated new fortunes, and exerted unprecedented political influence. Precise, uniform railroad time—the essence of the emerging industrial order—imposed a new regularity on the tempo of American life.

As early as the 1840s St. Louis entrepreneurs had recognized the potential of a national rail network, but they were losing regional initiative to Chicago by the eve of the Civil War. Local economic recovery after the war hinged on St. Louis becoming a regional rail hub as well as a river port. Businessmen bridged the Mississippi at St. Louis and tapped new trade territories to replace the Upper Midwest that Chicago had taken away. The very names of the crucial St. Louis rail lines—the St. Louis, Iron Mountain and Southern, the Missouri Pacific, the Missouri, Kansas and Texas, and the Texas and St. Louis—all indicated the city's new regional thrust (91).

The prize was the South and the Southwest, both poised for economic development after the devastation of the Civil War. The end of Reconstruction and the election of President Rutherford B. Hayes—both political deals sealed in part by railroad bribes and by the promise of federal railroad subsidies—paved the way for the interrelated rise of the New South and new St. Louis industries. Local manufacturers and railroad entrepreneurs were in the right place at the right time to jump at expanding southern markets, especially those west of the Mississippi River.

Cotton compressing was the leading example of a new, rail-dependent St. Louis industrial enterprise built on a southern commodity. Before the Civil War, St. Louis had not been an important cotton market because most deep-South cotton went downstream by river to Gulf Coast ports. After the war, when the cotton belt moved west into Arkansas, Oklahoma, and Texas, marketing became dependent on rail.

The St. Louis Cotton Exchange offered cash prizes to attract southern planters, and in 1875 local boosters hosted a national railroad convention to stake the city's claim on the trade. St. Louis quickly became the world's largest inland cotton market. Between 1866 and 1880 annual cotton receipts rose from 55,000 to 500,000 bales.

The problem was that shipping cotton by rail was relatively inefficient, and hence relatively expensive. The bulky bales filled up freight cars but left them far short of their weight-carrying capacity. The solution was to squeeze three-and-one-half-foot bales into dense blocks only nine inches high. Compressing increased transportation efficiency, making it cheaper to ship southwestern cotton to the East Coast by rail than by boat.

James Paramore established the first St. Louis cotton compress in 1873. *Pictorial St. Louis* showed the huge plant covering more than a block on the levee just south of Park Avenue (92). Efficiently designed and serviced by river as well as by rail, the compress was a model of modern, high-volume, industrial-flow technology. Standard bales from southern gins entered one end of the plant, passed through huge hydraulic presses, and came out the other end as flat blocks ready for shipment to distant textile mills.

Paramore's example encouraged other local cotton compress operations and supporting industries—especially railroads. In 1879 Paramore and his Cotton Exchange associates organized the Texas and St. Louis Railroad, aptly nicknamed the Cotton Belt Line, with the help of a federal land grant. The cotton trade contributed so much to the St. Louis economy that James Paramore became a local industrial hero. In 1880 friends and admirers presented him with an ornate sterling-silver service engraved with scenes that contrasted poor black sharecroppers in southern fields with modern compress technology in St. Louis. The soup tureen lid had a handle fashioned to look like a freight car, loaded with flattened cotton bales (93).

92. Above: St. Louis Cotton Compressing Company, *Pictorial St. Louis*

93. Left: Paramore soup tureen, 1880

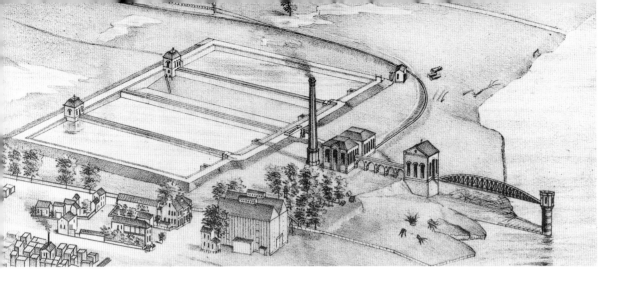

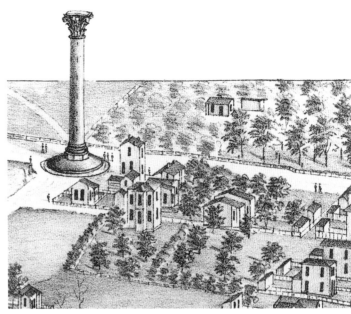

94. Above: Bissell's Point water works, *Pictorial St. Louis*

95. Above Right: North Grand Avenue water tower, *Pictorial St. Louis*

Networking

Underground pipes and overhead wires held the city together. More tangible than community sentiment and more permanent than politics, networks of water and gas mains, electric wires, and communications lines were the vital ligaments of urban life.

Infrastructure development in Gilded-Age St. Louis required not only technological expertise but also more capital than the city could raise. Since the 1840s, municipal government had taken responsibility for drinking water and drainage systems—and had nearly exhausted its resources in the process. By the 1870s, the city clearly needed more infrastructure than it could afford, and that need paved the way for private-sector development of public utilities. During the next quarter century, the city's expanding utility network evolved into a hodgepodge of public and private enterprises unevenly distributed across the urban landscape.

The networking effects of physical infrastructure were

often invisible or hard to understand. Pipes ran underground, out of sight, and it was virtually impossible to perceive any pattern in the maze of overhead utility wires. *Pictorial St. Louis* revealed few of the networks of water mains, sewers, gas lines, and telegraph wires that were tying St. Louis together by 1875. Separate lithographs showed the new Bissell's Point pumping station, the North Grand Avenue water tower, and the Compton Heights Reservoir as isolated structures rather than parts of an integrated, city-wide water system.

From the Bissell's Point water intake and mud-settling basins, located at the foot of Grand Avenue, huge steam-driven pumps sent the water uphill to the North Grand Avenue water tower (94). Designed in the style of an oversized Corinthian column by the city's premier architect, George I. Barnett, the 1871 tower was an impressive Gilded-Age effort to dress up modern technology in classical garb (95). The tower served as a shock absorber to smooth out the surge from the Bissell's Point pumps. From

the high tower, the water flowed downhill to the Compton Heights Reservoir, then into the network of water mains, and finally into the service lines of individual customers.

The system delivered muddy water, and too little of it, but in the late 1860s city leaders recoiled from the projected costs of a modern filtered water system. In the 1880s, chronically low water pressure and mounting demands for cleaner water forced the city to add more settling basins and a second water tower on Bissell Avenue, visible to the left of the Grand Avenue tower in an 1890 photograph taken from north of the towers (96). A decade later, a new pumping station at Chain of Rocks and a third water tower at Compton Heights increased both flow and pressure, but the still-unfiltered water remained as murky as ever.

Unlike the municipally owned water works, local electric power and communications utilities developed as highly competitive, privately owned "public" utilities. They began in the 1880s on a modest scale, with portable generators and small service networks fed by central power stations. Lucrative city contracts for street lighting, increasing demand for power to operate electric trolleys, and the growing popularity of domestic electric lighting attracted private investors, whose pooled capital paid for

ever-larger generators and more wiring. Cutthroat competition encouraged consolidation and the formation of utility monopolies. In the mid-'90s, St. Louis had more than seventeen electric utility companies; by 1902 the Union Electric Company had collapsed them into one.

Telegraph wires had been part of the local urban scene since the late 1850s, and by the '90s forests of utility poles lined downtown streets, bearing a tangle of telegraph, telephone, and electric power lines (98). In 1880 St. Louis Bell Telephone had six hundred subscribers, most of them businesses, and all St. Louis calls came through the company's single switchboard (97). As soon as the Bell patent expired in the mid-'90s, the rival Kinloch Telephone Company entered the field to compete for the growing residential trade. Before Southwestern Bell Telephone Company purchased the Kinloch system in 1922, St. Louisans who wanted full service had to install the phones of both companies. Eventually AT&T consolidated all American phone companies into a single national monopoly.

Physical infrastructure made the Gilded-Age city possible and allowed it to function. Though silent, often hidden from view, and easily ignored or taken for granted, utility networks structured and energized urban life.

96. Far Left: Bissell and North Grand water towers, 1890

97. Above: St. Louis Bell Telephone Company switchboard, 1884

98. Below: Sixth Street, c.1890

99. Above: Collier White Lead and Oil Company, *Pictorial St. Louis*

100. Above Right: Collier White Lead and Oil Company, 1878

Manufacturing

Manufacturing transforms raw materials and combines them into new products. Some manufacturing processes are relatively simple, but most involve complex technologies. While it is fairly clear how clay becomes brick or how a log becomes furniture, it is not immediately apparent how fermented grain produces beer or vinegar, or how vinegar converts metallic lead into paint pigment. Although hundreds of factories appear in *Pictorial St. Louis*, few of the sketches show the products they made, and fewer still reveal how they made them. The manufacturing processes themselves—the real creative forces that drove the industrial age—remain obscure.

Lead paint and lager beer suggest the variety of manufacturing processes under way in the Gilded Age. The combined effects of geology, geography, and culture explain why the city became famous for both. St. Louis was close to the lead mines and smelters of outstate Missouri, and its rapidly developing trade territory had limitless potential as a paint market. Lead-paint pigments were cheap, durable, and popular. Indeed, the primary colors of Gilded-Age America were the red and white of lead paint; everywhere red barns, railroad cars, bridges, and factory structures complemented white houses.

Lead paint was an ancient product, and medieval methods still prevailed in the vast corroding sheds of local white-lead works. At the Collier White Lead Company on Clark Avenue, workers placed lattice-like lead plates in ceramic pots of vinegar, stacked the pots ceiling-high, then covered them with stable waste—creating, in effect, huge manure compost heaps (99). Over a period of months the rotting compost generated heat and gases which accelerated the chemical reaction between the lead and the vinegar. The pots were then emptied and the white lead transferred to the main plant, where steam-driven mills ground it in linseed oil to become the white lead of commerce (100). Gilded-Age painters made their own paint on each job site by mixing pigments with linseed oil, turpentine, and chemical dryers; pre-mixed paints became available after 1867, but professional painters resisted their use.

Because every step in the manufacturing process exposed workers to lethal lead compounds, profits from lead pigments came at considerable social cost. Lead-furnace fumes and clouds of pigment dust constantly polluted local air, while spills and waste dumps contaminated soil and ground water. Lead poisoning was widely feared but little understood, because many of its symptoms were equally attributable to other causes.

Brewing was another ancient process. First, barley grain was sprouted or "malted" to produce an enzyme that could convert the starch in grain to sugar. Next, malted barley, grain, and hop leaves for flavoring were boiled together, cooled, and inoculated with yeast. Feeding on the sugar, the yeast gave off alcohol and carbon dioxide bubbles as waste products. The end result was beer. If the beer was popular German-style lager, it was then aged slowly in caves or ice houses.

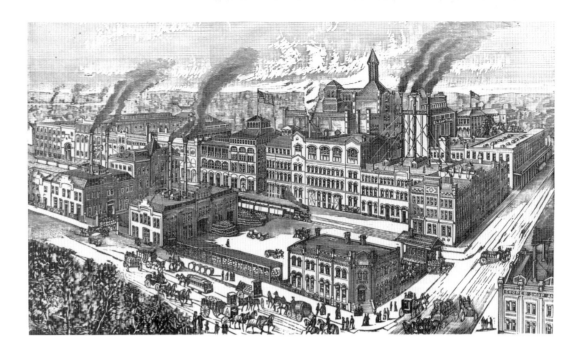

Gilded-Age innovations in beer-making, like lead-paint production, focused less on manufacturing methods than on increasing output and sales. In 1876 Adolphus Busch introduced Budweiser, a light-bodied lager designed as a national brand acceptable to all tastes (103). Busch's aggressive wholesaling required pasteurizing equipment, bottling works, and refrigerated railroad cars in addition to conventional brewing apparatus. An 1883 lithograph of the Anheuser-Busch complex conveys a much better impression of large-scale manufacturing in Gilded-Age St. Louis than do the *Pictorial St. Louis* views of traditional breweries, like Anthony and Kuhn's on Victor Street (101, 102).

101. Left: Anthony and Kuhn Brewery, *Pictorial St. Louis*

102. Above: The Anheuser-Busch Brewery, 1883

103. Right: One of the first Budweiser bottles, c.1876

Transformations: Manufacturing

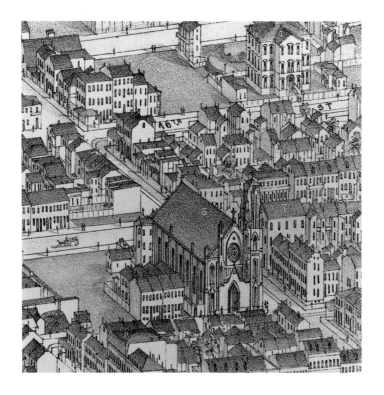

Schooling

Gilded-Age educators believed that the purpose of schooling, whether public or private, was to transform children into the kinds of adults their parents and community wanted them to be. They likened schools to factories that processed raw human nature into dutiful workers and respectful citizens. True to the principles of Horace Mann and other pioneers of American popular education, St. Louis schools strove for social control, not for individual self-realization.

Local schooling remained entirely private until the first public school opened in 1838. Even afterwards, most children of the well-to-do continued to attend private schools, where they learned the academic skills and social graces that defined their station. Less affluent St. Louisans sent their children to public schools or to neighborhood parochial schools that reinforced family religious beliefs and were often ethnically segregated. Separate schools prepared boys and girls for their separate roles as men and women. African-American schools were also separate—and unequal.

American-style public schools had been invented in the 1830s primarily to foster social cohesion in a nation of many peoples, faiths, and interests, but few unifying institutions or traditions. Educators hoped that common schooling—a universally shared experience during impressionable childhood years—would foster a common national culture.

As the population grew more diverse during the Gilded Age, public schooling became an even more urgent need. William Torrey Harris, superintendent of the St. Louis public schools from 1868 to 1888, developed a systematic, kindergarten-through-high school curriculum that became a national model for urban schooling in the industrial age.

Schools appear in almost every lithograph of *Pictorial St. Louis*, particularly in those views that show working-class districts where high population density and ethnic diversity required a multiplicity of public and parochial classrooms. In Camille Dry's view, the St. Lawrence O'Toole Roman Catholic school at 15th and O'Fallon was partially hidden by the church spire (104). Just a block north, at 16th and Cass, stood the twelve-room O'Fallon Public School, one of twenty-seven similar school buildings erected shortly after the Civil War to accommodate an expected flood of pupils.

Local educators had to work quickly and efficiently, because there were no compulsory attendance laws until the turn of the century. Only about half of all school-age

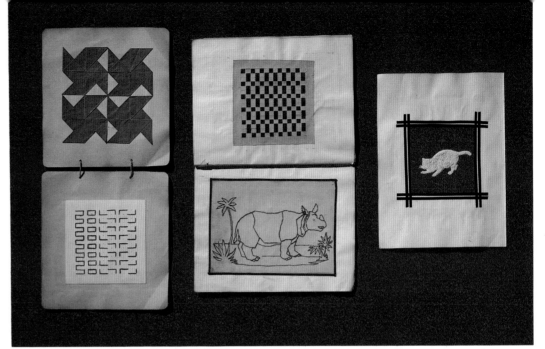

children regularly attended school in Gilded-Age St. Louis, and few remained in school once they were old enough to go to work. In 1880, three quarters of all public school students were clustered in the first three grades.

In 1873 Susan Blow, a Harris protégé and the daughter of a wealthy local industrialist, promoted kindergartens to give the schooling process a head start. Blow volunteered to train teachers in the Froebel method of pre-school education, developed in Germany, and to run a demonstration kindergarten at the Des Peres School in Carondelet (105). St. Louis kindergartens taught children self-control and obedience in a cheerful and supportive classroom environment. They learned small-motor control by mastering detailed, repetitive tasks—such as paper-weaving projects—that produced uniform results (106).

After kindergarten, elementary-age children proceeded

grade by grade through the rote-learned lessons of Superintendent Harris' highly structured curriculum. At ten o'clock in the morning on any given school day, every third-grader in every school in the city could be heard reciting the same lesson, in a classroom arranged just like all the others.

Elementary school graduates in the Gilded Age were well trained, though even they sometimes had trouble answering the questions on the public high school entrance exam (107). In 1890, high school students represented only 2 percent of the public school enrollment; most of them were women studying to be teachers. In any case, the really important lessons that most St. Louis children learned in school were not the three Rs, but the social, moral, and patriotic lessons of self-discipline and respect for authority.

107. Right: Sample high school entrance exam questions, 1879

105. Far Left: Des Peres School, 1876

106. Above: Kindergarten pattern books, c.1880

Shakespeare

I. Give an example, each, of words obsolete, obsolescent, changed in form, confined to poetical vocabulary, of infrequent usage, seemingly obsolete, but explicable by figure; mention phrase and play in which each occurs.

II. Illustrate what would now be a want of purity of diction, by mentioning one word used in a Latin sense, one word evidently French, one word Italian, and one word from Spanish.

108. Above: Brass box iron, c.1875

109. Above Right: Checkered Game of Life board game, c.1863

Prospering

Rags-to-riches success was a popular theme in Gilded-Age novels, but in real life most wealthy people had wealthy parents, and people born poor generally died poor. Although workers frequently changed jobs and dwellings in an attempt to better their condition, there was far more mobility within classes than between them. Opportunities for advancement most often came from new jobs in business or the professions and from the widening range of occupational choices offered by the expanding consumer economy.

The main beneficiaries of Gilded-Age material progress were urban dwellers who were better off than the working class but not yet well-to-do. These members of the emerging middle class had enough disposable income to buy homes and consumer goods and enough social aspiration to strive ever upward. The new middle class had fairly clear social boundaries, but its economic definition was imprecise because class identity involved more than income alone. Type of employment, living conditions, material possessions, family organization, social activities, and cultural style all distinguished the middle-class way of life. The Checkered Game of Life, a popular Gilded-Age board game for all ages, promoted middle-class values by rewarding thrift and diligence and by penalizing gambling and sloth (109).

Achieving and maintaining a middle-class home was a constant effort in which men and women had different but equally important roles. As men increasingly worked outside the home, women labored within it to nurture the social values and provide the material comforts of middle-class domesticity. The goal was a level of tasteful comfort that set the home apart from the drab quarters of mechanics and laborers without aping the ostentation of the newly rich. Trade cards, like this sewing machine ad, illustrate the close connections between consumption, man's responsibility to provide, woman's obligation to be useful and ornamental, and the goal of family happiness (110). Plain household appliances were good enough for servant use, but decorative versions, such as fancy brass irons, allowed the woman of the house to display her refined taste while she demonstrated her domestic skill (108). Indeed, the Gilded-Age cornucopia of affordable, mass-produced household goods made consumption virtually a full-time job, even a moral responsibility.

Caroline and Andrew Fruth, pictured on page 21, achieved middle-class status in Gilded-Age St. Louis. Andrew, a German immigrant, clerked in a southern Illinois dry goods store until he saved enough money to open a monument company in St. Louis with Henry Filsinger, a stonecutter. Henry ran the shop, while Andrew, an enterprising businessman, managed a corps of traveling salesmen who marketed tombstones in small towns on both sides of the Mississippi.

Three years after their marriage, the Fruths bought a house, shown in *Pictorial St. Louis*, in a developing neighborhood of modest single-family homes on Sidney Street (111). As his business grew over the next two decades, Andrew added to his savings, increased Caroline's household allotment, and steadily accumulated a houseful of furniture and modern conveniences. The Fruths also expanded their social circle; the women pictured here at formal tea on the lawn were Caroline's close friends (112).

As the German-American Fruths prospered over the years, they moved bit by bit into the mainstream American middle class. Andrew gradually began to keep his accounts in English; he and Caroline started joining clubs and attending theaters that were not exclusively German. They sent their son to Washington University to become a dentist, and in the 1890s they left Sidney Street for a grander home in newly developed, prestigious Compton Heights.

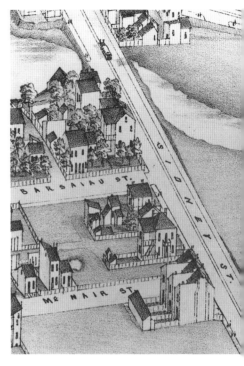

110. Above: Trade card, c.1885

111. Above Right: Fruth home (third row house, south [left] side of Sidney, east of McNair), *Pictorial St. Louis*

112. Below: Mrs. Emil Boehl's lawn party, 1880

Places

Places stand out from their surroundings, but they never stand alone. Each locale—however distinctive—remains embedded in a broader landscape. City places are especially responsive to the world outside their bounds; in crowded quarters every space impinges on another, and even private property has a public aspect because individual actions often have social consequences.

City places can be natural features or human artifacts, spaces or structures, formal or informal. They can be fixed landmarks, such as public markets, or channels of movement, like streets and alleys. Places change over time and sometimes become social metaphors, as in the case of the West End and North St. Louis. No single place can adequately sum up a whole city, but almost any place, examined in its broader context, can illustrate how events in one area affect what happens in another.

The west end of Lucas Place, detailed in *Pictorial St. Louis*, showed the forces of economic growth and social change contending against the power of place. Laid out in the 1850s, Lucas Place was an exclusive residential retreat for wealthy St. Louisans seeking refuge from industrial pollution, commercial hubbub, and immigrant neighbors. Restrictive deed covenants regulated land use inside the enclave and screened out undesirables—excluding, ironically, the very kinds of enterprises and people responsible for Lucas Place fortunes.

By 1875 Lucas Place was fully developed as far west as 18th Street and was filling up rapidly with substantial townhouses beyond 21st Street. Just east of 18th Street, between Lucas Place and Washington Avenue, stood Washington University and the Second Presbyterian Church, both prominent landmarks of the local elite (#15, #16).

The most puzzling section of Lucas Place was the undeveloped gap between 18th and 21st streets, still vacant except for a pond and a few barns and sheds. The cluster of buildings north of the pond, along Washington Avenue, probably explains why no one was eager to live there. The large structure at Washington and 21st was a streetcar stable (#12). The building complex next door and directly across Washington Avenue was Nicholas Schaeffer's Soap and Candle Factory (#11).

Noise from throbbing engines, rumbling streetcars, and neighing horses echoed through the area day and night; the stench from stable manure, coal smoke, rendering vats, and soap kettles poisoned the air. The 20th Street pond was a foul, industrial sink. Little wonder that no one had built on the immediately adjacent Lucas Place lots.

Wealth, private property, and deed restrictions were not enough to insulate Lucas Place from its urban surroundings. Industrial pollution spilled over from nearby factories; business, industry, and worker housing crowded in on every side. At the corner of Pine and 19th stood a large public skating rink, a mere block from Lucas Place—but a social class apart (#2).

113. Facing: Detail, Plate 54, *Pictorial St. Louis*

114. Right: House at 2728 Washington Avenue, c.1890

115. Far Right: The Terrys' neighborhood, *Pictorial St. Louis*

The West End

The area that Gilded-Age St. Louisans called the West End was the latest westward extension of the city's old central corridor. The West End consisted roughly of the eighteenth and twenty-eighth wards, created when St. Louis City and County split in 1876, but its boundaries were less definite than its character. Home to the local elite, the West End was an enclave of gracious dwellings and private streets that were spatially, economically, and socially segregated from the rest of the city.

Wealthy St. Louisans had been fleeing commercial and industrial expansion since before the Civil War, repeatedly abandoning their old city neighborhoods for new residential developments farther west along the central corridor. Relocation was a matter of individual choice, but it had a collective effect. The local elite moved ever westward as a group; with each migration, they transplanted their churches, schools, and social clubs. Over the years they developed increasingly elaborate land-use covenants and deed restrictions to protect their exclusive domains.

The 2700 block of Washington Avenue, between Beaumont Street and Leffingwell Avenue, was a fashionable West End address in 1870 when Albert Todd, a prominent attorney, bought the mansard-roofed townhouse at 2728 as a wedding present for his daughter, Elizabeth, and her husband, John H. Terry (114). The Terrys' house was one of the few city structures that Camille Dry sketched for *Pictorial St. Louis* but failed to finish; the unshaded roof made it hard to see behind the steeple of the Second Baptist Church. Dry did show the

116. Left: 2728 Washington Avenue, c.1900

117. Above: 2728 Washington Avenue, c.1950

118. Right: Washington Avenue, 3600 block, *Pictorial St. Louis*

neighborhood filled with pleasant, tree-lined streets and imposing, mainstream churches, both evidence of the taste and status of its residents (115).

Later views of 2728 Washington Avenue show its advancing age and the progressive decline of the neighborhood. The Terrys moved in 1880 and in the mid-'90s their bay window was removed to make space for a new house on the adjacent lot to the east. By the early twentieth century the iron fence and the stone entry posts were gone; a utility pole had replaced the maple tree, and the widening of Washington Avenue had taken some of the former curb space. The house next door to the west was for rent (116).

The elite had long since left the area by the 1950s. Many of the old townhouses were now rooming houses,

and their entryways had lost most of their original charm (117). The lot next door to the Terry house was vacant again. The west wall of their once-stylish dwelling now served as a gaudy billboard for Cleo Cola.

Pictorial St. Louis illustrated two stages in the process of residential development along Washington Avenue: the Terrys' 2700 block in its prime, and a new enclave just developing in the 3600 block between Grand and Vandeventer avenues (118). Within a few years this section of Washington Avenue also lost its luster, dooming nearby Vandeventer Place to a similar fate by the turn of the century. Once again wealthy St. Louisans fled west, this time to the apparent safety of West End private streets near Kingshighway and even beyond.

A Southside Block

Neighborhoods constantly change. Their boundaries, characteristics, and even their names shift over time as different residents come and go.

During the Gilded Age, the area that St. Louisans now call "Soulard" did not exist as a distinctive, named place. It was merely part of a larger, near-southside area that included land previously owned by Julia Cerré Soulard. Emil Boehl's 1872 photograph of Broadway north from Rutger Street shows one location in this part of the city: the shopping district between the Soulard Market and the South or "French" Market at Broadway and Chouteau Avenue, here visible just beyond the turn in the horsecar tracks (119).

Residents of the near south side were then predominantly German and Bohemian, Irish, and native-born black and white Americans. Indeed, no working-class district in St. Louis was home to only one ethnic or racial group; people of every heritage lived in every ward. Distinctive ethnic enclaves were usually small and short-lived, less often whole neighborhoods than blocks or partial blocks, buildings, or even single households. By 1880 an influx of Austrians, Croatians, Serbians, and other southern and eastern Europeans added even more cultures and languages to the local ethnic mix.

119. Above Left: Broadway north from Rutger Street, 1872

120. Left: Block bounded by Jackson, Carondelet, Soulard, and Lafayette, *Pictorial St. Louis*

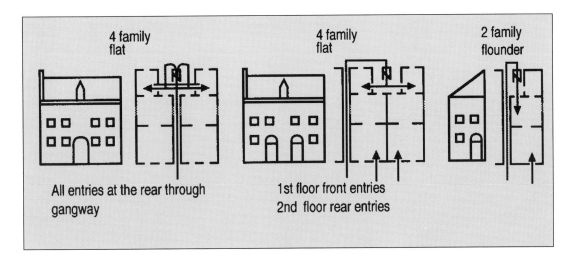

4 family flat

4 family flat

2 family flounder

All entries at the rear through gangway

1st floor front entries
2nd floor rear entries

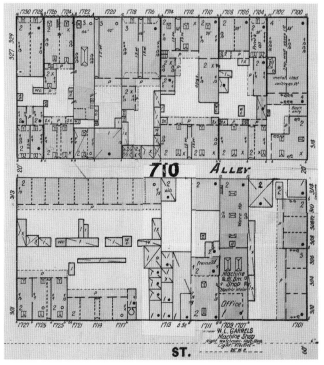

The block bounded by Jackson Street (later Third), Carondelet Avenue (later Broadway), Soulard Street, and Lafayette Avenue was typical of many near-southside blocks that appeared in *Pictorial St. Louis* (120). Densely packed two-story row houses—many with only half-gable roofs—nearly filled the block, and a second tier of back-yard dwellings faced the alley that cut through from north to south.

The four hundred people who shared this block in 1880 were a fair sampling of working-class St. Louis. One in six residents was black. Three-quarters claimed German birth or parentage, but few of the immigrants were newcomers; almost all their children under twenty were native born. More than half of the seventy-nine households had five members. Occupations varied: skilled trades predominated among the white men; white women washed and ironed, worked as domestics, or held factory jobs. Black men were porters, waiters, teamsters, and laborers, while black women washed and ironed. Half the boys and a quarter of the girls under twenty had jobs outside the home.

121. Above: Floor plans of typical working-class homes

122. Right: Whipple insurance map, 1892

Although most lots already had buildings when Camille Dry drew the block in 1875, owners continued to make additions and improvements. A color-coded, fire-insurance underwriter's map of the same area seventeen years later revealed the spatial arrangements and functions of every structure (122). Pink structures were brick; yellow structures were wood frame. Many of the brick buildings were multifamily flats, each consisting of three connected rooms with a front or rear entrance (121). Back yards were cluttered with coal sheds and privies, designated "WC" on the map, shared by many families. Some residents probably drew their drinking water from common faucets in the back yards, since many working-class flats lacked running water during the Gilded Age.

Places: A Southside Block   75

Separate Spheres, Proper Places

Expectations were different for men and women during the Gilded Age. According to the doctrine of "separate spheres," each gender had its special abilities and temperament, and hence its proper place and social role. The notion that men and women functioned best in separate—though sometimes intersecting—spheres was most clearly expressed in white, middle-class culture, but St. Louisans of every race, class, and income subscribed to this idea at some level of belief and behavior.

Separate spheres and proper places had spatial as well as ideological implications. Man's sphere was the workplace and the public places of economic and political power: office buildings, city hall, the Merchants' Exchange.

Less obvious were the masculine private places where powerful things got done. Men met informally at gentlemen's clubs and saloons, where regular patrons might have had their personalized beer steins prominently displayed behind the bar (123). Downtown hotels served as informal meeting places for civic leaders, local entrepreneurs, traveling salesmen, and their associates. Gathered around the billiard table in the lobby of the Southern Hotel, men could mix business with pleasure in an atmosphere free from female constraints (124). Women were not formally excluded from the public lobby, but there was nothing particularly welcoming about its décor or furnishings.

Woman's proper place was the home and its domestic extensions, the school, the church, and private charities. By doing volunteer work, by giving lessons at home or in school, or by taking in laundry or boarders, women could expand the range of paid and unpaid "women's work" and build extensive social networks, all within the bounds of propriety.

What most effectively expanded woman's sphere—in fact, even if not in theory—was Gilded-Age industrialism, which created a glut of new consumer goods and put money in the pockets of middle-class women. Retailers began to court female customers by deliberately creating places for women in the downtown business district, formerly a male preserve. Large department stores changed the character of downtown by

123. Above: Golden Lion beer stein

124. Right: Lobby of the Southern Hotel

vastly increasing the number of female workers and shoppers, who in turn created a demand for still more women's shops and services. By drawing more women into the public world of commerce, merchandizing helped erode the spatial separation of the sexes. Ultimately, all paying customers are equal.

The William Barr Company, launched in 1849 as a branch outlet for an East-Coast dry goods company, pioneered women's merchandizing in post-Civil War St. Louis. In 1875 Barr's narrow, four-story building fronted on fashionable Fourth Street where, as the firm's advertising noted, feminine feet loved to tread (127). Three years later, Barr demolished one of the few remaining mansions in the downtown area to build an even larger emporium. Barr's new department store gave women an opportunity to shop for the latest fashions while surrounded by amenities geared to their needs and interests. Like Crawford's, another early department store pictured here in an 1887 lithograph, Barr's had electric lighting, telephones, steam elevators, well-appointed dressing rooms, an inviting tea room, scheduled entertainments, and illustrated fashion catalogues, all aimed at enticing women downtown for a shopping adventure (125).

The resources of urban culture widened the range of personal choice, and many middle-class women were content to enjoy their opportunities without openly challenging the doctrine of separate spheres. Others stretched the limits of domesticity to include municipal housekeeping, becoming temperance, child-welfare, or clean-air activists. A few, like the suffragist Virginia Minor, overstepped the bounds by insisting that woman's place was also in the voting booth (126).

125. Above: Interior of Crawford's Department Store, 1887

126. Below: Virginia Minor, St. Louis suffragist, c.1885

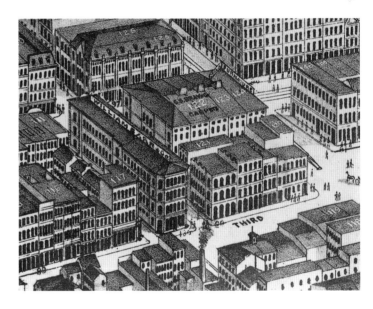

127. Above: William Barr Company, department store, *Pictorial St. Louis*

128. Left: Third Street Market, 1903

129. Below: South or "French" Market, *Pictorial St. Louis*

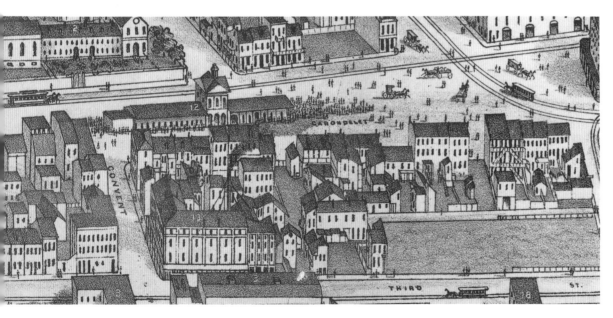

Public Markets

City people have to eat, but they cannot grow their own food. Urban life is impossible without a reliable system of food supply and distribution, especially of perishable meats, vegetables, and dairy products. The larger the city the greater the problem. Today, St. Louisans buy most of their groceries in supermarkets, but in the Gilded Age they shopped primarily in public markets. The difference between public markets and supermarkets measures a century of change in technology, merchandising, social policy, and eating habits.

Before the invention of electric refrigerators, freezers, microwave ovens, and processed, brand-name foodstuffs, household provisioning was a daily chore and a constant public concern. City governments regarded food supply as a kind of public utility, too vital to be left to the uncertainties of private enterprise. Instead, municipalities owned, managed, or regulated public markets in which private vendors leased selling space (128). In most cities, the principal market houses were large and imposing places, often second in size only to government buildings; they were located in residential districts near main transit lines for the convenience of shoppers who had to carry groceries home. Public markets rationalized urban food supply, policed retail trade practices, and drew more customers than any single vendor could otherwise attract. Intense competition kept food prices low. Specialized shops and small neighborhood corner groceries filled in whatever gaps remained in the food distribution system.

Public markets were much more than places to shop. Many had meeting halls, and all were focal points of neighborhood life, where residents mingled daily on a

130. Far Left: Center Market, *Pictorial St. Louis*

131. Left: Union Market, 1867

132. Below: Kirkwood Market, 1993

roughly equal basis to satisfy a common human need. In symbolic recognition of these markets' vital role, Camille Dry sketched the largest crowd visible anywhere in *Pictorial St. Louis* at the South or "French" Market on Broadway near Chouteau (129).

Dry also sketched twelve other public markets. Soulard, South, Center (130), Union (131), and Biddle were the largest, each an immense, block-long structure. No market was more than a few blocks from another, evidence of high downtown population density and heavy patronage by pedestrian shoppers.

In Gilded-Age St. Louis, public markets fostered a common urban culture, and their passing helped erode it. Only Soulard Market has survived twentieth-century suburbanization, home refrigeration, modern supermarkets, and fast food, to remind St. Louisans of the world they have lost. Ironically, county suburbs such as University City and Kirkwood have in recent years built new but old-style public markets in a conscious attempt to promote community feeling (132).

whole family. On Sunday afternoons, ethnic audiences flocked to hear German bands, choral groups, and musical productions at Anthony and Kuhn's, Hyde Park, Uhrig's, Stifel's, Schnaider's, and other major beer gardens (133).

Many Anglo-Americans disapproved of beer-garden sociability, especially on the Sabbath, and denounced the Germans' beloved institution as little better than a saloon.

The nearly 1,200 gathering places listed under "Saloons" in the 1875 *Gould's St. Louis Directory* ranged from beer gardens to bawdyhouses to the corner bars then proliferating in every working-class neighborhood. Men returning from work on the Franklin Avenue streetcar could get off at 17th Street, and in just a few steps be with their friends at any one of four saloons (135). Saloons became social clubs and political centers for working people.

133. Above: Schnaider's Beer Garden, c.1880

134. Above Right: Schnaider's Beer Garden, *Pictorial St. Louis*

135. Far Right: Franklin Avenue at 17th Street, *Pictorial St. Louis*

Gathering Places

Urban living brought diverse St. Louisans together every day on the job and in the street, but in their leisure hours they generally preferred to socialize with people like themselves. Throughout the city, the wide variety of gathering places reflected the residents' rich cultural diversity—and stubborn cultural exclusiveness.

For German St. Louisans, beer gardens represented the best of the old country transplanted to the new. Local brewers, who sold beer wholesale, also operated beer gardens on the brewery grounds (134). Often lavishly landscaped, beer gardens had outdoor tables and covered pavilions; some owners even built bandstands and performing stages. They offered good food and local lager, music, pinochle, and respectable conviviality for the

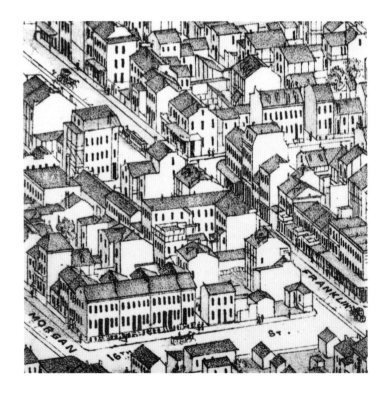

Only a mile southwest of the Franklin Avenue saloons, but a world apart, stood the spacious Pine Street quarters of the exclusive University Club. While working men met over beer and pickled eggs in the Franklin Avenue saloons, professional men met at the University Club to discuss business over cigars and fine wines (137).

Distinctions of social class, race, and ethnicity most often kept St. Louisans apart, but sometimes they met on common ground to enjoy community-wide entertainment. The annual Agricultural and Mechanical Fair, a local fall tradition since 1856, drew thousands to the fairgrounds west of Grand Avenue. St. Louisans also loved to parade, seizing almost any opportunity to march behind the banners of their various clubs and voluntary associations. Paradoxically, the most exclusive public event of all, the business elite's annual parade of the Veiled Prophet, was also the most popular. At least for one night each year, St. Louisans forgot their differences and gathered together on downtown sidewalks to cheer the floats and marvel at the dazzling "illuminations" (136).

136. Left: Veiled Prophet Parade, 1880

137. Above: University Club of St. Louis, c.1890

Continuities

SAINT LOUIS IN THE GILDED AGE

The past fades but never quite goes away. It persists in artifacts, institutions, habits, and memories, but especially in structures and the physical landscape. These relics of the past are both tangible and symbolic; they touch our sentiments as well as our interests, sometimes as a heritage, sometimes as a burden.

If we look backward at *Pictorial St. Louis* from the vantage point of the late twentieth century, it becomes evident that the Gilded Age was the dawning era of our own times. The city that took shape then is the foundation of the city we live in now. The character of the population has changed several times since Camille Dry walked the streets with his sketch pad, but most of those streets and a surprising number of the structures he drew still remain. Modern visitors can still find their way around the north side near Hyde Park using *Pictorial St. Louis* as a guide. There is still a fire station on the southeast corner of the park, although the nineteenth-century building was replaced in the 1920s (#6). The Evangelical Lutheran Bethlehem Church school building, built in 1872, is still there, but a 1927 tornado removed the top half of the adjoining church building (#8, #7).

The confines of urban space intensify the dynamics of social change and highlight the tension between past and present. Cities are places that extend the range of individual choice—but always within the bounds of historical and geographical possibility. The interplay between time, space, place, and people sets the historical stage, casts the players, and directs the action.

The past remains a potent force because our current notions of what is and ought to be stem largely from our understanding of what used to be. We live not only with material reminders of St. Louis in the Gilded Age, but also with values, attitudes, and expectations passed on from that generation to ours. We are as concerned now as Gilded-Age St. Louisans were then about the city's problems and prospects; we still ponder, as they did a century ago, the meaning of progress, fairness, and social responsibility.

138. Facing: Detail, Plate 76, *Pictorial St. Louis*

TOWER GROVE PARK.

Public Parks

The large public parks of St. Louis, like those of most other major American cities, are legacies of the Gilded Age. Planned and landscaped to meet the social needs of increasingly crowded industrial cities, these parks were quite different from the open spaces St. Louisans had used for outdoor activities since colonial times. Gilded-Age city parks were more "public" than ever before. Because they were municipally owned, the citizens who used them became involved in decisions affecting their use. In a democratic but culturally diverse community, there was no end to public debate over who should use city parks and for what purposes.

The novel idea that prime urban space should be reserved for public use came from several sources: eighteenth-century European parks; early nineteenth-century American cemeteries such as St. Louis' own park-like Bellefontaine; and especially Frederick Law Olmstead's trend-setting New York Central Park, completed in the 1860s. These new city parks were designed to give the laboring classes some breathing space and to cultivate civic virtue through exposure to nature improved by landscaping and art.

The first St. Louis parks mixed public ownership with private control. In 1844 the city dedicated part of the old southside common fields as Lafayette Park. Residents of the surrounding fashionable neighborhood paid to fence the park and plant a few trees, but it remained primarily a parade ground until 1866, when the city issued bonds to purchase ornamental iron benches, a Chinese pagoda, and a bandstand. A police station was also added to preserve public order in the increasingly popular park.

In 1868 Henry Shaw, a land speculator and retired hardware merchant, presented the city with Tower Grove Park, adjacent to his country home, just west of the city limits. A detail from *Pictorial St. Louis* shows some of the park's amenities—similar to those of Lafayette Park—and a portion of the landscaping that made it such an exquisite Victorian walking park (139). Henry Shaw furnished the heroic statuary, contrived classical ruins, and weekly band concerts to elevate the taste of the masses (140). St. Louisans less interested in moral uplift visited the popular lion pool, bear pits, and amusements at Fairgrounds Park, far to the north but better served by streetcars (142).

The crown jewel of the local park system was Forest Park, a 1,370-acre tract west of Kingshighway purchased by the city in 1874 and incorporated within the city limits two years later. The 1875 plan for Forest Park featured some of the latest fashions in municipal park design: meandering trails, carriageways, and promenades; deep woods and open glades; picturesque scenic vistas opening at every turn; and a hippodrome track where gentlemen could race their carriages (141).

Over the next century, Forest Park changed with changing public needs and desires. Even if World's Fair construction crews had not felled most of the original forest, Forest Park would doubtless still have become less rural, open, and woodsy, and more devoted to popular sports, such as golf, baseball, and tennis, that required dedicated space.

In the twentieth century, Forest Park became the home of cultural institutions that vied for park land with people who enjoyed the freedom of open spaces. Legally it remains the property of the city, which by the 1990s could ill afford to repair or replace aging infrastructure. Today, Forest Park is still public space shared by St. Louis City and County residents, who debate endlessly how best to use and maintain their legacy from the Gilded Age (143).

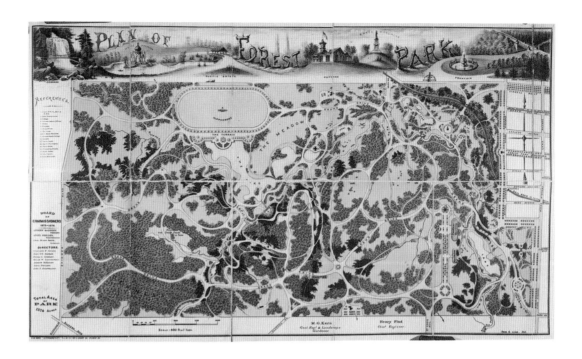

141. Top: Map of Forest Park, c.1875

142. Above: Fairgrounds Park sea lion pool, c.1875

143. Right: The History Museum, Forest Park, 1993

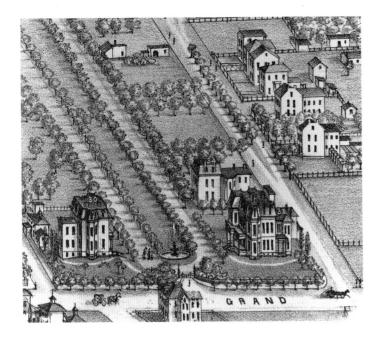

144. Above: Vandeventer Place, *Pictorial St. Louis*

145. Above Right: Vandeventer Place from the east, 1880

Private Places

Nineteenth-century industrial cities were filthy, noisy, and congested. In the absence of zoning laws that would keep stores and factories out of residential districts, citizens had little hope of ensuring clean and healthful surroundings short of fleeing to the salubrious suburbs.

Wealthy St. Louisans, even more than the elite of other American cities, sought private solutions to the public problem of environmental quality. During the Gilded Age, they used the private place to insulate themselves from the surrounding city. Private places were subdivisions; instead of becoming public thoroughfares, their streets remained privately owned and controlled by the adjacent property owners. Private-place residents funded their own infrastructure; they also regulated property ownership and use with restrictive deed covenants.

Real estate developers, recognizing that homeowners would pay extra for a chance to control their surroundings, laid out exclusive, attractive enclaves such as Vandeventer Place, located just west of Grand Avenue (144). In 1870 Charles Peck and Julius Pitzman, both experienced developers, laid out its eighty-six lots around a tree-lined parkway filled with pools and fountains. Peck built his own mansion just inside the tasteful, wrought-iron entry gates that advertised Vandeventer Place's exclusivity (145). Restrictive covenants outlawed commercial buildings, churches, and schools within the compound and set the minimum dwelling cost at 10,000 dollars.

Within twenty years, however, the constant rumble of electric trolleys along Grand Avenue signaled a change in the surrounding neighborhood. Vandeventer Place residents barricaded themselves behind new fortress-like gates, but to no avail (147). The once-fashionable enclave declined rapidly after the turn of the century; in 1950, what was left of Vandeventer Place, including Charles Peck's by-then derelict mansion, was razed to make way for Cochran Veterans' Memorial Hospital.

Later private-place promoters learned from earlier mistakes as they laid out Portland and Westmoreland Places west of Kingshighway. Instead of platting single-street developments, so vulnerable to change, they grouped several private streets into larger neighborhoods and guarded the core of residential lots with buffers of park land and luxury apartments (148).

Not only did private places become notable features of the local landscape; they also served as powerful symbols of local attitudes toward urban space and civic responsibility. Perfected in the Gilded Age by the well-to-do, private places legitimated a popular urge toward residential retreat and isolation which was later replicated in middle-class suburbs. St. Louis County suburban communities are still laced with private streets (146). The courts have outlawed most of the socially restrictive deed covenants, but the form and function of the places remain to assert the primacy of private over public interest, and the continuing local inclination to seek individual solutions to community problems.

146. Left: Private street, University City, 1993

147. Below Left: East gates, Vandeventer Place, c.1920

148. Below: Plat map of Portland Place and Westmoreland Place, c.1890

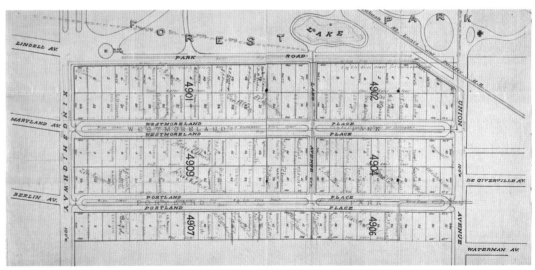

Eads Bridge

T he Eads Bridge is unobtrusive. The weathered stone piers blend into the levee landscape, the gentle arches spring low to the water, and no superstructure rises above the road deck. Unlike the nearby Gateway Arch, Eads Bridge neither shimmers nor soars.

Nevertheless, for more than a century St. Louisans have taken this masterpiece of Gilded-Age engineering as a civic icon, the prime relic of their past, a symbolic bridge to their future (149). Residents instantly recognize the triple-arch profile. Arches remain perennial motifs in local public art and advertising graphics, and they echo in the architecture of such diverse structures as the Jefferson National Expansion Memorial, the Lambert International Airport terminal, and Busch Stadium (150).

In 1874 James Eads closed his final report as chief bridge engineer with the hope that his structure would endure as a noble monument to his times. Even more than he realized, the Eads Bridge embodied the character of Gilded-Age St. Louis: flashy civic optimism, entrepreneurial verve, technological audacity, and capitalist wheeling and dealing.

For a time in the twentieth century it seemed that the Eads Bridge had outlived its usefulness. The road and rail decks had remained busy as long as the bridge was the only local Mississippi crossing and as long as large numbers of St. Louisans commuted daily to east-side suburbs (152). Beginning in the 1890s, however, a succession of rival bridges drained away first rail and later truck and auto traffic. Eventually, trains became too heavy for the aging bridge and too wide to fit through the tunnel connecting it to the Mill Creek Valley train yards. The last train crossed in July 1974, a century after the

149. Below: Artist's concept of west abutment, Eads Bridge, 1874

150. Below Right: Advertisement with Eads Bridge motif, c.1880

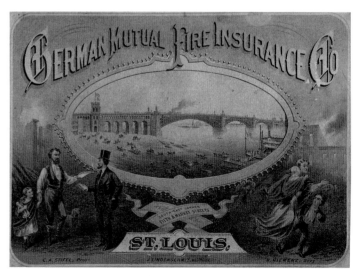

first. All but a useless, rusting hulk, the Eads Bridge stood in historical limbo: too sturdy to fall down, too expensive to keep up, too precious to abandon (153).

What revived the bridge was the same impulse that had inspired it: the realization that a metropolis is ultimately no more successful than its transportation infrastructure. As the automobile age entered its closing phase in the late twentieth century, the need for energy-efficient, metropolitan area-wide mass transit became ever more urgent. Planners hoped that MetroLink, a regional light-rail system combined with feeder-bus routes, would successfully link the city and surrounding counties. Built to run on existing railroad rights-of-way, MetroLink rail cars cross the Eads Bridge and run through the old rail tunnel under downtown streets before exiting near Busch Stadium. The first phase connecting East St. Louis with Lambert Airport opened in 1993 (151).

For the first time in a quarter century St. Louisans can again cross the Eads Bridge on the train deck and rediscover—or discover for the first time—the hidden

151. Above Left: MetroLink crossing Eads Bridge, 1993

152. Above: East entrance to Eads Bridge, c.1903

153. Right: Detail of Eads Bridge superstructure, 1974

excitement and artistry of their most notable historical artifact. They can share the secret, long known only to trainmen and derelicts, that the Eads Bridge has not only an imposing outside but also a dramatic inside. Its superstructure and road deck form the walls and ceiling of a 1,500-foot corridor where the curves of the arches play tricks with perspective and the latticework of steel girders creates intricate patterns of light and shade.

Always beautiful and now useful once again, the Eads Bridge endures as James Eads hoped it would: a symbol of the city and a legacy from his times to ours.

Sumner High School

Racism runs deep throughout St. Louis history. Slavery arrived with the founding families and remained a feature of daily life until the Civil War. The war brought liberation—most local slaves deserted their masters before formal emancipation in 1865—but not equality. The Thirteenth Amendment left African Americans trapped somewhere between bondage and liberty, legally free but still chained by custom and prejudice.

Determined to keep African Americans separate and unequal, white St. Louisans imposed various forms of legal and de facto segregation, especially Jim Crow housing, schools, and public accommodations. Racially segregated private organizations reinforced public policy. Segregation had a dual effect on black St. Louisans, throwing them back on their own resources as it kept them apart. Within the constraints imposed by prejudice, local African Americans created their own institutions and community life.

Sumner High School was a product of determined African-American self-help. In 1867 the city opened free public schools to African Americans, and in the early 1870s it operated six small, unnamed elementary schools for a black population that had increased from 3,000 in 1860 to 22,000 by 1870. When state law mandated an African-American high school in 1875, the school board opened Sumner High School as a combined elementary and high school in the old Washington School building at Spruce and Eleventh streets (155). Black parents and community leaders unsuccessfully objected to the site, earlier deemed unsuitable for white students because of the nearby railroad yards, factories, bawdyhouses, and the city jail, which was housed in the municipal courts building across Spruce Street (154).

Although African Americans lived in every ward of the city, their greatest concentration was in the central wards east of Grand Avenue. In 1877 almost half of all black children enrolled in public school went to Sumner. That year the school board bowed to community pressure led by Charlton H. Tandy, a black political activist, and hired its first black teachers, all trained at the new Lincoln University in Jefferson City. Sumner High School added its own Normal School for teacher training in 1890.

Worn down by the unrelenting efforts of black parents and ministers, the St. Louis School Board eventually assigned names to the African-American schools, upgraded their buildings, and brought the curriculum into line with that of the white schools. On the whole, St. Louis black public school teachers were better trained than their white counterparts and more involved with their students. Black schools had smaller classes, and some teachers supplemented the standard curriculum with after-hours manual-training instruction.

Sumner graduated its first two high school students in

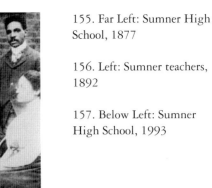

155. Far Left: Sumner High School, 1877

156. Left: Sumner teachers, 1892

157. Below Left: Sumner High School, 1993

1885. Thirty-three of the 130 students who had graduated by 1894 went on to the Normal School to become teachers themselves (156). In the twentieth century, the growing corps of Sumner-trained teachers and other professionals became the self-renewing foundation of the local African-American middle class.

By the mid-'90s, numerous black middle class families had moved west of Grand Avenue, particularly into the area north of Easton Avenue known as Elleardsville. In 1896 three hundred black citizens petitioned to move Sumner High out of its downtown slum neighborhood and closer to its potential student body. The school board first relocated Sumner to another old white public school building at Washington and 14th, then in 1910 to an imposing new facility in Elleardsville, by then popularly known as the Ville.

Anchored by Sumner High School, the Ville became the center of local African-American middle-class culture and home to many black business, religious, and civic leaders, most of whom were Sumner graduates. An outstanding faculty and strong community support made Sumner one of the premier African-American high schools in the nation and for years one of the best public high schools in the city.

Although legal school segregation ended in 1954, Sumner High still serves a black student body justly proud of its long tradition of academic excellence and community involvement. It remains a monument to the determination of oppressed people to improve their lives in spite of the barriers of racism (157).

An Ink-ling which seems to be a Dail(e)y occurrence in the County Court.

158. Above: Farmland near 1876 city limits, *Pictorial St. Louis*

159. Above Right: Cartoonist's impression of County Court session, 1870

City Limits

Some boundaries are natural features, others human artifacts. Some are easily changed or overcome, others persist across the generations. The history of any city charts the ongoing interplay between the various boundaries—geographical, political, and cultural—that divide and organize urban space.

Since colonial times St. Louis has been hemmed in by the Mississippi River on the east, and since the Gilded Age by the city limits on the west (158). The river is a natural barrier, difficult to bridge, while the city-county boundary is merely a line on a map. Yet this artificial boundary has proved to be no less an obstacle to metropolitan development. Separating St. Louis City from St. Louis County made good short-term sense in 1876, but in the twentieth century the division, frozen into law and buttressed by vested interests, has made it almost impossible for either city or county residents to address their interrelated problems of central city decline and suburban dispersal.

St. Louis City was part of St. Louis County until 1876. County legislators, then called the County Court, had wrangled over taxes and patronage for years. Joseph Keppler captured the spirit of this legislative body in his 1870 satiric cartoon (159). Although nine out of ten county residents then lived inside the city limits, east of Grand Avenue, county officials still controlled the purse strings. Voters hoped that by separating the urban area from the rural county, everyone would have more efficient government, more appropriate services, and lower taxes (160). The separation plan, known as the Scheme and Charter, increased the area of the city from eighteen to sixty-one square miles and gave St. Louis a home-rule charter that enabled it to function as a separate county.

Futuristic granite sculptures today mark the 1876 city-limits line where it crosses Manchester Road, Delmar Boulevard, and other major thoroughfares, but otherwise there are few visible clues to its course. The line traces a long arc from the southern edge of Carondelet to Bellefontaine Neighbors, with a narrow extension

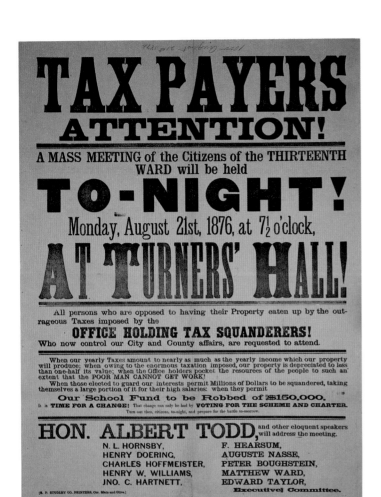

160. Far Left: Announcement of meeting to support city-county separation, 1876

161. Left: Blanchette Memorial Bridge to St. Charles, 1993

162. Below: Poplar Street Bridge to Metro East, 1993

400,000 live in St. Louis; one million live in St. Louis County, two-thirds of them in ninety separate municipalities. Although voters have approved special city-county taxing districts for cultural institutions, transportation, and sewage treatment, for the most part they remain as unwilling as their forebears to address regional needs.

Few people today believe that St. Louis City and County will ever reunite. The wealthier county spurns union with the poorer city; African Americans, who are close to a majority in the city, do not want to dilute newly acquired political power. Meanwhile, people are voting with their cars, streaming east and west across the old geographical and political boundaries (161, 162). Nearly two-and-a-half million people live in a nine-county metropolitan area in Missouri and Illinois, but only 57 percent of them in either St. Louis City or County. The city that industrialism transformed in the Gilded Age is searching for a new role in the decentralized, interdependent metropolis that now stretches beyond its limits.

northward along the Mississippi just beyond the I-270 bridge at Chain of Rocks. From south to north, it follows the west bank of the River Des Peres to Shrewsbury, then proceeds north roughly parallel to McCausland, Skinker, and Goodfellow.

When they ratified "The Great Divorce" in 1876, St. Louisans believed a million residents would one day live within the city limits. Today, however, fewer than

Notes on Sources and Suggestions for Further Reading

Saint Louis in the Gilded Age derives its content and interpretive thrust from the collections of the Missouri Historical Society and from recent scholarship. Most of the scholarly articles on St. Louis have appeared in either the *Missouri Historical Society Bulletin* (*MHSB*), *Gateway Heritage* (*GH*), or the *Missouri Historical Review* (*MHR*). For others, see the comprehensive periodical bibliography, *America: History and Life*. In addition to these and other sources, the essays draw on the collections of the Missouri Historical Society, contemporary newspapers, St. Louis city directories, and the Tenth Census of the United States, 1880.

The Great Metropolis of the Mississippi Valley

Articles in the *Journal of Urban History*, and the following interpretive studies helped place Gilded-Age St. Louis in comparative context, and contain extensive bibliographies:

Sam Bass Warner, Jr., *The Urban Wilderness: A History of the American City* (New York, 1972); David R. Goldfield and Blaine A. Brownell, *Urban America: A History* (2d ed., Boston, 1990); Nell Irvin Painter, *Standing at Armageddon: The United States, 1877-1919*

(New York, 1987); Alan Trachtenberg, *The Incorporation of America: Culture and Society in the Gilded Age* (New York, 1982); John Brinckerhoff Jackson, *American Space: The Centennial Years, 1865-1876* (New York, 1972); Daniel E. Sutherland, *The Expansion of Everyday Life, 1860-1876* (New York, 1989); Thomas J. Schlereth, *Victorian America: Transformations in Everyday Life, 1876-1915* (New York, 1991); Eric H. Monkkonen, *America Becomes Urban: The Development of U.S. Cities and Towns, 1870-1980* (Berkeley, 1988); Stuart Weems Bruchey, *Enterprise: The Dynamic Economy of a Free People* (Cambridge, 1990); Raymond A. Mohl, *The New City: Urban America in the Industrial Age, 1860-1920* (Arlington Heights, 1985).

Especially helpful studies of other cities include Sam Bass Warner, Jr., *The Private City: Philadelphia in Three Periods of Its Growth* (Philadelphia, 1968); Richard C. Wade and Harold M. Mayer, *Chicago: Growth of a Metropolis* (Chicago, 1969); Theodore Hershberg, ed., *Philadelphia: Work, Space, Family, and Group Experience in the Nineteenth Century: Essays Toward an Interdisciplinary History of the City* (New York, 1981); William Cronon, *Nature's Metropolis: Chicago and the Great West* (New York, 1991); Samuel P. Hays, ed., *City at the Point: Essays on the Social History of Pittsburgh* (Pittsburgh, 1989).

There are relatively few histories of St. Louis. The most comprehensive for the Gilded Age are James Neal Primm, *Lion of the Valley, St. Louis, Missouri* (2d ed., Boulder, Colo.,

1990) and Katharine T. Corbett, Howard S. Miller, Mary Seematter, and Alex Yard, "Labor, Capital, and Culture: St. Louis in the Industrial Age," *St. Louis in American History*, Unit 6, a Missouri Historical Society curriculum project in publication. The focal point of the exhibition and the book is Camille N. Dry and Richard J. Compton, *Pictorial St. Louis: A Topographical Survey Drawn in Perspective* (St. Louis, 1876). Other useful contemporary accounts are William Hyde and Howard L. Conard, *Encyclopedia of the History of St. Louis: A Compendium of History and Biography for Ready Reference* (New York, 1899); James Cox, *Old and New St. Louis: A Concise History of the Metropolis of the West and Southwest, with a Review of Its Present Greatness and Immediate Prospects* (St. Louis, 1894); and J. Thomas Scharf, *History of St. Louis and St. Louis County, from the Earliest Periods to the Present Day: Including Biographical Sketches of Representative Men* (Philadelphia, 1883). Logan Uriah Reavis, *Saint Louis, The Future Great City of the World* (St. Louis, 1870) is the best example of Gilded-Age booster rhetoric.

Modern editions of influential contemporary works referred to in the text are Mark Twain and Charles Dudley Warner, *The Gilded Age: A Tale of Today*, Bryant M. French, ed. (New York, 1972); Edward Bellamy, *Looking Backward, 2000-1887* (New York, 1960); Henry George, *Progress and Poverty* (New York, 1984); Josiah Strong, *Our Country: Its Present Perils and Future Promise*, Jurgen Herbst, ed. (Cambridge, 1963).

The primary inspiration for this book came from cultural geography and landscape studies. For a comprehensive bibliography see Michael P. Conzen, Thomas A. Rumney, and Graeme Wynn, eds., *A Scholar's Guide to Geographical Writing on the American and Canadian Past* (Chicago, 1993). The following proved particularly helpful: John Brinckerhoff Jackson, *The Necessity for Ruins, and Other Topics* (Amherst, 1980), and *Discovering the Vernacular Landscape* (New Haven, 1984); Ervin Zube, ed., *Landscapes: Selected Writings of J.B. Jackson* (Amherst, 1970); Donald W. Meinig, ed., *The Interpretation of Ordinary Landscapes: Geographical Essays* (New York, 1979); Grady Clay, *Close Up: How to Read the American City* (New York, 1974); David Buisseret, ed., *From Sea Charts to Satellite Images: Interpreting North American History Through Maps* (Chicago, 1990); Carville Earle, *Geographical Inquiry and American Historical Problems* (Stanford, 1992); Gerald A. Danzer, *Public Places: Exploring Their History* (Nashville, 1987).

Perspectives

On maps and bird's-eye urban views as historical sources, see John W. Reps, *Views and Viewmakers of Urban America: Lithographs of Towns and Cities in the United States and Canada, Notes on the Artists and Publishers, and a Union Catalog of Their Work, 1825-1925* (Columbia, 1984), and *Saint Louis Illustrated: Nineteenth-Century Engravings and Lithographs of a Mississippi River Metropolis* (Columbia, 1989); Denis Wood and John Fels, *The Power of Maps* (New York, 1992); Mark S. Monmonier, *How to Lie with Maps* (Chicago, 1991); David Buisseret, *Historic Illinois from the Air* (Chicago, 1990), and *From Sea Charts to Satellite Images*, cited above. On photographs as historic sources, see Peter B. Halyes, *Silver Cities: The Photography of American Urbanization, 1839-1915* (Philadelphia, 1984); Alan Trachtenberg, *Reading American Photographs: Images as History* (New York, 1989); Alan Thomas, *Time in a Frame: Photography and the Nineteenth-Century Mind* (New York, 1977). On the physical appearance of Gilded-Age St. Louis, see Julian S. Rammelkamp, "St. Louis in the Early Eighties," *MHSB* 19 (April 1963); George McCue, Osmund Overby, and Norbury L. Wayman, "Street Front Heritage: The Bremen/Hyde Park Area of St. Louis," *MHSB* 32 (July 1976); John Kouwenhoven, "Downtown St. Louis as James B. Eads Knew It When the Bridge Was Opened a Century Ago," *MHSB* 30 (April 1974); Quinta Scott and Howard S. Miller, *The Eads Bridge* (Columbia and London, 1979); Lawrence Lowic, *The Architectural Heritage of St. Louis, 1803-1891: From the Louisiana Purchase to the Wainwright Building* (St. Louis, 1982); Carolyn Hewes Toft, *St. Louis: Landmarks & Historic Districts* (St. Louis, 1988).

Landscapes

On the city in relation to its region and rivers, see Timothy R. Mahoney, *River Towns in the Great West: The Structure of Provincial Urbanization in the American Midwest, 1820-1870* (Cambridge, 1990); Philip V. Scarpino, *Great River: An Environmental History of the Upper Mississippi, 1890-1950* (Columbia, 1985); James H. Madison, ed., *Heart Land: Comparative Histories of the Midwestern States* (Bloomington, 1988); Allan G. Bogue, *From Prairie to Corn Belt: Farming on the Illinois and Iowa Prairies in the Nineteenth Century* (Chicago, 1963); Michael P. Conzen, ed., *The Making of the American Landscape* (Boston, 1990); James R. Shortridge, *The Middle West: Its Meaning in American Culture* (Lawrence, 1989); Michael P. Conzen and Kay J. Carr, eds., *The Illinois and Michigan Canal National Heritage Corridor: A Guide to Its History and Sources* (DeKalb, 1988). Relevant works on local landscape change over time include Charles E. Petersen, *Colonial St. Louis: Building a Creole Capital* (St. Louis, 1949); Virginia Anne Henry, "The Sequent Occupance of Mill Creek Valley" (M.A. thesis, Washington University, 1947); Helen D. and Joseph Vollmar, Jr., "Caves, Tunnels and Other Holes Under St. Louis," *GH* 8 (Fall 1987); Andrew Hurley, "Railroads and Real Estate in Antebellum St. Louis," *GH* 13 (Spring 1993); Eric T. Sandweiss, "Construction and Community in South St. Louis, 1850-1910" (Ph.D. dissertation, University of California, Berkeley, 1991); Ronald Grim, "How Old Surveys Shaped Today's Landscape," *Our American Land: 1987 Yearbook of Agriculture* (Washington, D.C., 1987).

Transformations

On *process* as a historical phenomenon, see Sigfried Giedion, *Mechanization Takes Command: A Contribution to Anonymous History* (New York, 1948); Lewis Mumford, *Technics and Civilization* (New York, 1934); and Daniel Boorstin, *The Americans* (3 vols., New York, 1958-73).

Edward C. Kirkland, *Industry Comes of Age: Business, Labor, and Public Policy, 1860-1897* (New York, 1961); David A. Hounshell, *From the American System to Mass Production, 1800-1932: The Development of Manufacturing Technology in the United States* (Baltimore, 1984); George Rogers Taylor and Irene D. Neu, *The American Railroad Network, 1861-1890* (Cambridge, 1956); James Arthur Ward, *Railroads and the Character of America, 1820-1887* (Knoxville, 1986); Alan R. Pred, *The Spatial Dynamics of U.S. Urban Industrial Growth, 1800-1914: Interpretive and Theoretical Essays* (Cambridge, 1966); and David F. Noble, *America By Design: Science, Technology, and the Rise of Corporate Capitalism* (New York, 1979) analyze the rise of Gilded-Age urban industrialism. C. Vann Woodward, *The Origins of the New South, 1877-1913* (Baton Rouge, 1951); Pete Daniel, *Breaking the Land: The Transformation of Cotton, Tobacco, and Rice Cultures since 1880* (Urbana, 1985); and Thomas Charlton, "The Development of St. Louis as a Southwestern Commercial Depot, 1870-1920" (Ph.D. dissertation, University of Texas-Austin, 1969) explain why St. Louis trade turned southwest after the Civil War. Susan Strasser, *Satisfaction Guaranteed: The Making of the American Mass Market* (New York, 1989) analyzes the origins of modern marketing and consumerism.

There is little modern scholarship on industrial development in Gilded-Age St. Louis. The best overviews are Primm, *Lion of the Valley* and Corbett et al., *St. Louis in American History,* Unit 6. The best accounts of local brewing and lead paint manufacture are Stanley Wade Baron, *Brewed in America: A History of Beer and Ale in the United States* (Boston, 1962), and William Pulsifer, *Notes for a History of Lead: And an Inquiry into the Development of White Lead and Lead Oxides* (New York, 1888). For accounts of individual firms, see Compton and Dry, *Pictorial St. Louis,* and Hyde and Conard, *Encyclopedia of the History of St. Louis.* An excellent nontechnical history of lead toxicity is Richard P. Wedeen, *Poison in the Pot: The Legacy of Lead* (Carbondale, 1984).

On urban infrastructure, see *The Mayor's Message with Accompanying Documents* (St. Louis, 1870-95); John P. Dietzler, "Sewerage and Drainage in St. Louis, 1764-1954" (M.A. thesis, St. Louis University, 1954); Sam Bass Warner, *Streetcar Suburbs: The Process of Growth in Boston, 1870-1900* (Cambridge, 1962); Stanley Schultz and Clay McShane, "To Engineer the Metropolis: Sewers, Sanitation, and City Planning in Late Nineteenth Century America," *Journal of American History* 65 (1978); Martin V. Melosi, *Garbage in the Cities: Refuse, Reform, and the Environment, 1880-1980* (College Station, 1981); Nelson M. Blake, *Water for the Cities: A History of the Urban Water Supply Problem in the United States* (Syracuse, 1956); Joel Tarr, "Infrastructure and the City Building Process in Pittsburgh in the 19th and 20th Centuries," in Hays, ed., *City at the Point;* Jessica H. Foy and Thomas J. Schlereth, eds., *American Home Life, 1880-1930: A Social History of Spaces and Services* (Knoxville, 1992); and David T. Beito and Bruce Smith, "The Formation of Urban Infrastructure through Nongovernmental Planning: The Private Places of St. Louis, 1869-1920," *Journal of Urban History* 16 (1990). Suggestive works on the new electric technologies include Richard Duboff, "The Telegraph in Nineteenth Century America: Technology and Monopoly," *Comparative Studies in Society and History* 26 (1984); Harold L. Platt, *The Electric City: Energy and the Growth of the Chicago Area, 1880-1930* (Chicago, 1991); David E. Nye, *Electrifying America: Social Meanings of a New Technology, 1880-1940* (Cambridge, 1990); Carolyn Marvin, *When Old Technologies Were New: Thinking About Communication in the Late Nineteenth Century* (New York, 1988); Wolfgang Schivelbusch, *Disenchanted Light: The Industrialization of Light in the Nineteenth Century* (Berkeley, 1988); and Claude S. Fischer, *America Calling: A Social History of the Telephone to 1940* (Berkeley, 1992). On infrastructure politics, see Jon C. Teaford, *The Unheralded Triumph: City Government in America, 1870-1900* (Baltimore, 1984); Robin L. Einhorn, *Property Rules: Political Economy in Chicago, 1833-1872* (Chicago, 1991); and Primm, *Lion of the Valley.*

The *Annual Reports* of the St. Louis Board of Education during the Gilded Age illuminate Gilded-Age schooling as a social process, as do the following studies: Paul S. Boyer, *Urban Masses and Moral Order in America, 1820-1920* (Cambridge, 1978); David Tyack and Elizabeth Hansot, *Managers of Virtue: Public School Leadership in America, 1820-1980* (New York, 1982); Selwyn K. Troen, *The Public and the Schools: Shaping the St. Louis System, 1838-1920* (Columbia, 1975); Ronald D. Cohen, "Urban Schooling in the Gilded Age and After," *Journal of Urban History* 2 (1976); Selma Berrol, "Urban Schools: The Historian as Critic," *Journal of Urban History* 8 (1982); Sarah van Ausdal, "A Case Study in Educational Innovation: The Public Kindergarten in St. Louis" (Ph.D. dissertation, Southern Illinois University-Edwardsville, 1985).

On the rise of the urban middle class, see Olivier Zunz, *Making America Corporate, 1870-1920* (Chicago, 1990) and Stuart Blumin, *The Emergence of the Middle Class: Social Experience in the American City, 1760-1900* (Cambridge, 1989). Studies of middle-class material culture include Gwendolyn Wright, *Moralism and the Model Home: Domestic Architecture and Culture Conflict in Chicago, 1873-1913* (Chicago, 1980); Asa Briggs, *Victorian Things* (Chicago, 1989); Harvey Green, *The Light of the Home: An Intimate View of the Lives of Women in Victorian America* (New York, 1983); and Thomas J. Schlereth, ed., *Cultural History and Material Culture: Everyday Life, Landscapes, Museums* (Ann Arbor, 1990).

Places

Excellent analyses of city places include the works of John Brinckerhoff Jackson and Grady Clay, cited above; Gunther Barth, *City People: The Rise of Modern City Culture in Nineteenth-Century America* (New York, 1980); David Schuyler, *The New Urban Landscape: The Redefinition of City Form in Nineteenth-Century America* (Baltimore, 1986); Myron A. Marty and David E. Kyvig, *Nearby History: Exploring the Past Around You* (Nashville, 1982); and Danzer, *Public Places*. For description, but no analysis, of public markets, see Philip Taylor, *A Brief History of the Public Markets and Private Markets Referred to as Public Markets in the City of St. Louis, Missouri* (St. Louis, 1961).

On the process and character of suburbanization, see Kenneth T. Jackson, *Crabgrass Frontier: The Suburbanization of the United States* (New York, 1985); Margaret Marsh, *Suburban Lives* (New Brunswick, 1990); Gwendolyn Wright, *Building the Dream: A Social History of Housing in America* (New York, 1981); and Scot McConachie, "Public Problems and Private Places," *MHSB* 34 (January 1978).

Working-class St. Louis in the Gilded Age awaits its historian, but Alexander Yard, "Workers, Radicals, and Capitalists: The St. Louis Strikes of 1877" (M.A. thesis, University of Missouri-St. Louis, 1976), and David Roediger, "Not Only the Ruling Class to Overcome, But Also the So-Called Mob: Class, Skill and Community in the St. Louis General Strike of 1877," *Journal of Social History* 19 (1985) point research in the right directions.

Broad-ranging studies of working-class culture include Herbert Gutman, *Work, Culture and Society in Industrializing America: Essays in American Working-Class and Social History* (New York, 1976); David Montgomery, *The Fall of the House of Labor: The Workplace, the State, and American Labor Activism, 1865-1925* (Cambridge and New York, 1987); David Ward, *Poverty, Ethnicity, and the American City, 1840-1925: Changing Conceptions of the Slum and Ghetto* (Cambridge, 1989); John Bodnar, *The Transplanted: A History of Immigrants in Urban America* (Bloomington, 1985); Lisabeth Cohen, "Embellishing a Life of Labor: An Interpretation of the Material Culture of American Working Class Homes, 1885-1915," in Thomas J. Schlereth, ed., *Material Culture Studies in America* (Nashville, 1982); Roy Rosenzweig, *Eight Hours for What We Will: Workers and Leisure in an Industrial City, 1870-1920* (Cambridge and New York, 1983); James Borchert, "Urban Neighborhood and Community: Informal Group Life, 1850-1970," *Journal of Interdisciplinary History* 11 (1981); Roy Rosenzweig, "The Rise of the Saloon," in Chandra Mukerji and Michael Schudson, *Rethinking Popular Culture* (Berkeley, 1991); Mary Ann Clawson, "Fraternal Orders and Class Formation in the Nineteenth-Century United States," *Comparative Studies in Society and History* 27 (1985); Nell Irvin Painter, *Exodusters: Black Migration to Kansas after Reconstruction* (New York, 1977); David Roediger, *The Wages of Whiteness: Race and the Making of the American Working Class* (London and New York, 1991). For specific St. Louis studies see Gary Ross Mormino, *Immigrants on the Hill: Italian-Americans in St. Louis, 1882-1982* (Urbana, 1986); Audrey Olson, *St. Louis Germans, 1850-1920: The Nature of an Immigrant Community and Its Relation to the Assimilation Process* (New York, 1980); Gary R. Kremer, Antonio F. Holland, and Lorenzo J. Greene, *Missouri's Black Heritage* (Rev. ed., Columbia, 1993).

For urban gender roles see William Leach, "Transformations in a Culture of Consumption: Women and Department Stores," *Journal of American History* 71 (1984); Carroll Smith-Rosenberg, *Disorderly Conduct: Visions of Gender in Victorian Society* (New York, 1985); Susan Porter Benson, *Counter Cultures: Saleswomen, Managers, and Customers in American Department Stores, 1890-1940* (Urbana, 1986); Susan Strasser, *Never Done: A History of American Housework* (New York, 1982); Catherine E. Beecher and Harriet Beecher Stowe, *The American Women's Home: or, Principles of Domestic Science* (New York, 1971); Margaret Marsh, "From Separation to Togetherness: The Social Construction of Domestic Space in American Suburbs, 1840-1915," *Journal of American History* 76 (1989); and Laura Staley, "Suffrage Movement in St. Louis in the 1870s," *GH* 3 (Spring 1983).

Continuities

David Lowenthal, *The Past is a Foreign Country* (Cambridge and New York, 1985); Jo Blatti, ed., *Past Meets Present: Essays About Historic Interpretation and Public Audiences* (Washington, 1987); and Warren Leon and Roy Rosenzweig, eds., *History Museums in the United States: A Critical Assessment* (Urbana, 1989) thoughtfully explore how Americans relate to their past. For recent reflections on the continuing influence of the past on local contemporary affairs, see George Lipsitz, *The Sidewalks of St. Louis: Places, People and Politics in an American City* (Columbia, 1991) and James E. O'Donnell, ed., *St. Louis Currents: The Community and Its Resources* (St. Louis, 1992).

Roy Rosenzweig and Elizabeth Blackmar, *The Park and the People: A History of Central Park* (Ithaca, 1992) provides a broader context for Carolyn Loughlin and Catherine Anderson, *Forest Park* (Columbia, 1986). Beito and Smith, "The Formation of Urban Infrastructure"; McConachie, "Public Problems and Private Places"; and Sandweiss, "Construction and Community in South St. Louis" set the private place phenomenon in context.

Scott and Miller, *The Eads Bridge*, and the *St. Louis Post-Dispatch Magazine*, July 25, 1993, recount the long decline and recent rebirth of the bridge as part of the MetroLink regional light rail system. Sumner High School deserves a major historical study. In the meantime see St. Louis Public Schools, *Annual Reports*, and Lawrence O. Christianson, "Black St. Louis: A Study in Race Relations, 1865-1916" (Ph.D. dissertation, University of Missouri-Columbia, 1972). On St. Louis City-County separation see Thomas S. Barclay, *The St. Louis Home Rule Charter of 1876, Its Framing and Adoption* (Columbia, 1962); William N. Cassella, "City-County Separation: 'The Great Divorce' of 1876" *MHSB* (January 1959); and Susan Glassman, "Local Governments," in O'Donnell, ed., *St. Louis Currents*.

List of Illustrations

Unless otherwise noted, all images and artifacts are from the collections of the Missouri Historical Society. Items designated MHS-L are from the Library Collection; MHS-M, the Manuscripts Collection; MHS-MC, the Museum Collections; and MHS-PP, the Photograph and Print Collection. All object photography by Bob Kolbrener, unless otherwise noted.

1. "Map of the Territory in the Above Perspective," lithograph, Richard J. Compton and Camille N. Dry, *Pictorial St. Louis: A Topographical Survey Drawn in Perspective* (Compton and Company: St. Louis, 1876). MHS-L.

2. Plate 2, *Pictorial St. Louis*, 1876. MHS-L.

3. James B. Eads, photo by John A. Scholten, 1869. MHS-PP.

4. Title page, *Pictorial St. Louis*, 1876. MHS-L.

5. Eads Bridge under construction, photo by Robert Benecke, 1874. MHS-PP.

6. Pig flask, Anna Pottery, Anna, Illinois, 1888. MHS-MC.

7. Coffee tin, Johnson-Allen Coffee Company, c.1890. MHS-MC.

8. Brass inkwell, c.1874. MHS-MC.

9. Lamp from Merchants' Exchange Building, c.1875. MHS-MC.

10. Steam engine, late nineteenth century. Courtesy of Corporate Archives, Anheuser-Busch Companies, Inc.

11. Trade card, Bryan, Brown and Company, c.1880. MHS-PP.

12. Wedding bonnet made by Mary Deneny, c.1880. MHS-MC.

13. Banner, St. Louis Butcher-Verein, 1906. MHS-MC.

14. Adding machine, American Arithmometer Company, 1903. Courtesy of Jefferson County [Illinois] Historical Society.

15. Cigar store Indian, c.1870. MHS-MC.

16. "City of St. Louis: The City Limits at Various Periods," artist unknown, c.1955. MHS-L.

17. McLean Building, northeast corner of 4th and Market, photo by Emil Boehl, c.1875. MHS-PP.

18. Washington Avenue, west from 6th Street, photo by Emil Boehl, 1891. MHS-PP.

19. Singleton Street, photo by Thomas J. O'Reilly, 1892. MHS-PP.

20. Mule car next to trolley, unknown photographer, c.1890. MHS-PP.

21. Electric fan, Emerson Electric Company, 1895. Courtesy of Dr. William Hoehn.

22. Plant stand, c.1870. MHS-MC.

23. Hair wreath framed with photographs, 1876. MHS-MC.

24. Eastlake-style side chair, c.1880. MHS-MC.

25. Crazy quilt made by Mrs. Louis S. Barada, c.1890. MHS-MC.

26. Assemblage of wool flowers in glass dome, made by Louisa Hackman, c.1850. MHS-MC.

27. Caroline B. Fruth, photo by Boehl and Koenig, c.1880. Courtesy of Doris Stude.

28. Andrew Fruth, photo by Boehl and Koenig, c.1880. Courtesy of Doris Stude.

29. Lounge, c.1885. MHS-MC.

30. Toy graniteware, c.1880. MHS-MC.

31. Poorhouse dorm, photo by R.H. Fuhrmann, 1901. Courtesy of Ward Parker.

32. Cast-iron hall tree, c.1875. MHS-MC.

33. Bandolier, Ancient Order of Hibernians, late nineteenth century. MHS-MC.

34. Banner, Mystic Order of the Veiled Prophet, 1882. MHS-MC.

35. Beer stein, Cherokee Brewery Company, late nineteenth century. MHS-MC.

36. Member of Freie Gemeinde in fraternal attire, photo by Studio Hegyessy, c.1890. MHS-PP.

37. "Remarkable Exodus of Negroes...," etching, *Frank Leslie's Illustrated Weekly*, April 19, 1879. MHS-PP.

38. St. Liborius statue, late nineteenth century. Courtesy of New Holy Trinity Catholic Church

39. Sewing circle, c.1890. Proetz Collection. Courtesy of Western Historical Manuscripts Collection, University of Missouri-St. Louis.

40. Photographic baseball card of Charles Comiskey, Goodwin & Company, New York, c.1888. MHS-PP.

41. Workers at Platt and Thornburgh Paint and Glass Company, unknown photographer, c.1890. MHS-PP.

42. "An Unpaved Yard on North Eighth Street," halftone, Housing Committee of the St. Louis Civic League, *Housing Conditions in St. Louis* (St. Louis, 1908). MHS-L.

43. "St. Louis, Missouri," tinted wood engraving by Schell and Hogan after C.A. Vanderhoof, 1876. Courtesy of A.G. Edwards and Sons, Inc.

44. African-American stereotype mechanical bank, Shepard Hardware Company, Buffalo, N.Y., 1883. MHS-MC.

45. Irish stereotype mechanical bank, 1958 reproduction of 1875 cast-iron bank. MHS-MC.

46. "Look Here," lithograph, 1874. MHS-PP.

47. North Grand Avenue water tower, photo by Katharine T. Corbett, 1993.

48. Detail, Plate 45, *Pictorial St. Louis,* 1876. MHS-L.

49. Detail, Plate 2, *Pictorial St. Louis,* 1876. MHS-L.

50. Eads Bridge, photo by Robert Benecke, 1874. MHS-PP.

51. Detail, Plate 1, *Pictorial St. Louis,* 1876. MHS-L.

112. Mrs. Emil Boehl's party, photo by Emil Boehl, c.1880. MHS-PP.

113. Detail, Plate 54, *Pictorial St. Louis*, 1876. MHS-L.

114. John H. Terry residence, 2728 Washington Avenue, photo by Howard Terry, c.1890. MHS-PP.

115. Detail, Plate 71, *Pictorial St. Louis*, 1876. MHS-L.

116. Washington Avenue, 2700 block, unknown photographer, c.1910. MHS-PP.

117. Washington Avenue, 2700 block, unknown photographer, c.1950. MHS-PP.

118. Detail, Plate 85, *Pictorial St. Louis*, 1876. MHS-L.

119. Broadway north from Rutger Street, photo by Emil Boehl, c.1872. MHS-PP.

120. Detail, Plate 5, *Pictorial St. Louis*, 1876. MHS-L.

121. Floor plans, drawing by Becki Huntley, 1993.

122. Block 710, *A. Whipple's Insurance Maps*, vol. 1 (St. Louis, 1892), p. 8. MHS-L.

123. Golden Lion beer stein, late nineteenth century. MHS-MC.

124. Lobby of the Southern Hotel, lithograph, artist unknown, c.1865. MHS-PP.

125. "The Leading Dry Goods House of the West" (Crawford's Dry Goods Store), lithograph, *Rollingpin's Illustrated Exposition Street Parades and G.A.R.* (St. Louis, 1887). MHS-PP.

126. Steel engraving of Virginia Minor in Elizabeth Cady Stanton, Susan B. Anthony, and Matilda Joslyn Gage, eds., *History of Woman Suffrage* (New York, 1881-[1922]), vol. 2. Courtesy of St. Louis University Library.

127. Detail, Plate 21, *Pictorial St. Louis*, 1876. MHS-L.

128. Third Street Market, unknown photographer, 1903. MHS-PP.

129. Detail, Plate 3, *Pictorial St. Louis*, 1876. MHS-L.

130. Detail, Plate 24, *Pictorial St. Louis*, 1876. MHS-L.

131. Union Market, photo by Robert Benecke, 1867. MHS-PP.

132. Kirkwood Market, photo by Lorrie Calabrese, 1993.

133. Schnaider's Beer Garden, stereo photo by Robert Benecke, c.1880. MHS-PP.

134. Detail, Plate 40, *Pictorial St. Louis*, 1876. MHS-L.

135. Detail, Plate 43, *Pictorial St. Louis*, 1876. MHS-L.

136. "St. Louis Fair, Procession of the Veiled Prophet," wood engraving after photo by John A. Scholten, 1880. MHS-PP.

137. University Club of St. Louis, unknown photographer, c.1890. MHS-PP.

138. Detail, Plate 76, *Pictorial St. Louis*, 1876. MHS-L.

139. Detail, Plate 94, *Pictorial St. Louis*, 1876. MHS-L.

140. Columbus statue, Tower Grove Park, photo by Emil Boehl, 1886. MHS-PP.

141. "Plan of Forest Park," lithograph by Camille Dry, 1875. MHS-PP.

142. Fairgrounds Park sea lion pool, unknown photographer, c.1870. MHS-PP.

143. The History Museum, Jefferson Memorial Building, photo by Lorrie Calabrese, 1993.

144. Detail, Plate 85, *Pictorial St. Louis*, 1876. MHS-L.

145. Vandeventer Place from the east, photo by Emil Boehl, 1880. MHS-PP.

146. Private street, University City, Missouri, photo by Lorrie Calabrese, 1993.

147. East gates of Vandeventer Place, unknown photographer, c.1920. MHS-PP.

148. "Map of Griswold Tract: plat of land now comprising Westmoreland and Portland Places," 1890. MHS-L.

149. "The West Abutment of the Illinois and St. Louis Bridge," wood engraving by J.H. Kimbault, c.1874. MHS-PP.

150. Enameled tray, advertisement for German Mutual Fire Insurance Company, c.1874. MHS-PP.

151. MetroLink train crossing Eads Bridge, photo by Jerry Naunheim, Jr., 1993. Courtesy of *St. Louis Post-Dispatch*.

152. East entrance to Eads Bridge, photo by Emil Boehl, c.1903. MHS-PP.

153. Detail of Eads Bridge, photo by Quinta Scott, 1974.

154. Detail, Plate 23, *Pictorial St. Louis*, 1876. MHS-L.

155. Sumner High School, photo by Emil Boehl, 1877. Courtesy of St. Louis Public Library.

156. Sumner High School faculty, unknown photographer, 1892. Courtesy of Western Historical Manuscripts Collection, University of Missouri-St. Louis.

157. Sumner High School, photo by Bill Stover, 1993.

158. Detail, Plate 96, *Pictorial St. Louis*, 1876. MHS-L.

159. "An Ink-ling which seems to be a Dail(e)y occurrence in the County Court," lithograph by Joseph Keppler, *Die Vehme*, March 12, 1870. MHS-L.

160. "Taxpayers Attention!" broadside, R.P. Studley Company, 1876. MHS-M.

161. Poplar Street Bridge, photo by Larry Block, 1993.

162. Blanchette Memorial Bridge, photo by Larry Block, 1993.